General Phil Sheridan

and the Union Calvary

General Phil Sheridan
and the Union Calvary

By
Milton Lomask

Illustrated by Jo Polseno

HILLSIDE EDUCATION

Cover and interior book design by Mary Jo Loboda

Cover image: *Sheridan's Ride* By Thure de Thulstrup
(REPOSITORY: Library of Congress Prints and Photographs Division Washington, D.C. 20540 USADIGITAL ID:, Public Domain, https://commons.wikimedia.org/w/index. php?curid=2949221)

ISBN: 978-0-9976647-0-6

Hillside Education
475 Bidwell Hill Road
Lake Ariel, PA 18436
www.hillsideeducation.com

CONTENTS

General Phil Sheridan

and the Union Calvary

★ ★ ★ ★ ★ ★ ★ ★ ★ ★ ★ ★ ★ ★

1

THE CANNON

Opening his eyes with a start, Little Phil wasn't sure whether he had dreamed the distant booming sound that had awakened him or whether he had really heard it. From force of habit he started to nudge his brother. Then he remembered.

Mike wasn't with him this morning and the other bed in the little room hadn't even been slept in. Yesterday his three brothers and the younger of his two sisters had gone north to spend a month with their father in a construction workers' camp on the outskirts of Lancaster, Ohio.

Phil's father was a contractor. He was helping build the roads and the canals that every day were making it easier for the farmers of the Northwest to ship their grain to the cities of the East. John Sheridan's work kept him away for long intervals from his home in the little town of Somerset, Ohio. So the children took turns visiting him. The rule was that at least one boy must always remain with their mother, to chop wood for the kitchen range; to help tend the chickens, the pig, the horse ; and to milk the cows.

Phil yawned and stretched the sleep out of his joints. His eyes roamed the familiar room. His slowly shifting gaze took in the dresser with its cracked mirror, the wooden wall pegs where he and his brothers were supposed to hang their clothes, the chairs over which they actually threw them.

Facing east, the single window framed a corner of the orchard. Phil could pretty well gauge the time by the position of the sun on the floor. It stood at the third crack, meaning that the hour was somewhere between five and six. Getting-up time was six. He would know when it came because then the bells would ring out in the steeple of St. Mary's Church on Academy Hill.

Phil was having a debate in his mind—rise now or wait— when the distant booming sound reached his ears once more. It was real then. He hadn't dreamed it! The sound came again, shaking the bed and sending a shiver of delight through its small occupant.

He was out from under the sheet in a single movement, into his overalls and shirt in another. There was water in a basin on the dresser, soap beside it, towels on the rack against the wall. He made sparing use of all three and hastened into the kitchen.

The kitchen was also the family living room. It was a fine, bright room. Through four large windows, the morning sun splashed over the round pine table with its bow-back chairs, over the apple slices drying on strings along the rafters, over the little bookcase holding, among other things, a copy of the *Lives of the Saints,* Pike's *Arithmetic* and the bottle of allpurpose medicine which Mrs. Sheridan purchased from

Phil made sparing use of the weater, soap and towels.

a peddler every spring and which tasted so vile that Phil had long since sworn off being sick.

Mrs. Sheridan was already busy about the place. She had been for some time, judging by the smells. A new-baked pie was just coming out of the oven. With a dish towel protecting her hands, she was bearing it to the table as her son entered.

She smiled, a big, flashing smile. Mary Meenagh Sheridan was a woman with a laugh in her. She was swift in her movements, emphatic in her speech and firm in her opinions. Such were her ways—ways she had brought with her from County Cavan, Ireland. There both she and her husband had lived most of their years. From thence they had come to America along about the time of Phil's birth, not quite a decade earlier.

She would have spoken but her son was ahead of her.

"The cannon, Mama!" he shouted. "The six-pounder on Reading Hill. They're firing it this morning. Don't you hear it?"

"Don't I hear it indeed!" A chuckle raced through Mrs. Sheridan's words. "Three times now it has assaulted my eardrums. It's deafened we'll be before the morning's gone."

"But why?" The boy shot a puzzled glance at the calendar hanging next to the old beaver pelt above the fireplace. "They don't ever use it except on special occasions. Surely it's not yet the Fourth of July."

"For shame, boy! 'Tis the feast of your namesake, St. Philip Neri. Or if it's dull figures you want, consult the calendar."

This the boy was already doing, stretching a little to bring the numbers within range. The day was Tuesday, May 26, 1840.

His mother, returning to her stove, pulled open the oven door. "Be an angel," she said, "and fetch me the towel that I dropped there on the table in my great forgetfulness."

He fetched it and out came another pie. Like the first, it

was a cinnamon-scented masterpiece.

The boy trotted beside his mother as she carried it to the table. "Then why?" Tugging at her apron. "There must be some reason for firing the cannon."

"Reason enough. There's going to be doings in Somerset today."

"Real doings?"

"There's to be red-white-and-blue bunting on all the buildings and speechifying at the hotel. Leastwise so I've been told."

"Told, Mama? Who told you?"

"Our neighbor, Mrs. Ritchie."

Back to her stove went Mrs. Sheridan, this time remembering to take the towel. In a halo of fragrant goodness a third pie was removed from the oven and taken over to rest beside the others.

"Mrs. Ritchie came by last night," she explained. "This was after you and your sister had gone to bed. It's Mrs. Thomas Ritchie I'm referring to, the one whose husband has the big farm. It's running for Congress he'll be one of these days, or so they say. Not that I care about that, having no great consuming interest in the shenanigans of the Democrats."

Mrs. Sheridan's lilting speech ground to an abrupt finish. She looked around rather vaguely. "Now where was I?" she inquired.

"The celebration. You were talking about that. What's the reason for it?"

"There's a grand man coming to town on the twelve o'clock stagecoach—a man of great fame and distinction."

"Fame and distinction." Phil lingered over the words. "What's he famous for?"

"Well now—" Mrs. Sheridan cocked her head to one side.

She often did this and it always meant that some interesting idea had struck her. Apparently this one amused her. She smiled broadly. "Suppose now you stir your brains a little," she suggested. "I'll give you three guesses."

Three guesses! A game, eh! Fun! Phil gave his mother the eye. "Is he very famous?"

"Ver-r-r-y." The "r's" rolled. However long gone Mary Sheridan was from County Cavan, County Cavan was not yet gone from her.

"A general, Mama?"

"Grander than that!"

Thought, hard thought, made a latticework of Phil's brow. What, he wondered, could be grander than a general? An explorer perhaps, a famous Conestoga-wagon driver?

His thoughts took sudden flight, scattered by a sharp exclamation from his mother. Dropping her hands on his shoulders, she gave him a twirl that brought them face to face.

"Philip Henry Sheridan!" She rapped out each of his names like a drumbeat. "Is it to Mass you'll be going with that face? Is there no water in the bowl on your dresser?"

"Sure there is."

"Am I to conclude then that you've made no use of it at all?"

"I washed my hands and face good—with soap."

"Ah yes. Now that I look very close I can see the places. Here and here!" Mrs. Sheridan's forefinger lightly tapped two widely spaced spots on her son's cheeks. "For the rest I see nothing but high-water marks. Back to your room now and give yourself a scrubbing."

"But after we get back from Mass, after breakfast, I'll be working in the woodshed. I'll only get dirty all over again."

"I know of no law says you cannot wash twice in the same day. Begone now, and when you return let it be with a neck that's visible to the naked eye."

Phil did as he was told. Swinging into his room, he could hear his mother calling out behind him: "Everything. Understand me now! Face, ears, neck! And rinse—do you hear me, rinse! I want no acre of rich Ohio soil on the towel when you've finished."

Phil scrubbed and rinsed, and thought dark thoughts, having to do with the unreasonable ways of mothers.

When he regained the kitchen, his mother was no longer alone. His sister Mary had come out of the other bedroom. She was setting the table for the breakfast they would have on their return from Mass.

Mary was the oldest of the six Sheridan youngsters. Tall, willowy, with lovely complexion and clear blue eyes, she was womanly at thirteen. Phil's greeting to her was a large wink, which she gave back.

Mary was his special pal. Only she knew how many times he had played hooky during the previous school year. She was the only member of the family who had even the remotest idea how many fights he had got into. Into her ears, and hers alone, he had poured the story of what he and his pal, Hank Greiner, had done this very month on the last day of school.

At sunrise that morning, Phil and Hank had pried open one of the windows of Somerset's one-room schoolhouse. Climbing in, they had placed a large can of water on the inside mantel of the door. Then, climbing out again and closing the window behind them, they had crouched beneath it, waiting—and hoping.

All had gone according to plan. Mr. Mc-Manly, the spindly-legged schoolmaster, was alone when he unlocked the door. The can of water, dislodged as he strode in, tumbled with a loud splash. Outside, the two boys pummeled one another in glee, delighted at the sight of the startled look on the schoolmaster's face, the windmill movement of his arms as he brushed at his dripping frock coat.

Of course the boys were caught. Such pleasures must be paid for, and Mr. McManly was not noted for his teaching abilities. His fame rested on his skill with a hickory stick.

Having greeted his sister, Phil turned his mind again to the game he and his mother were playing. The man for whom the cannon was being fired—what could he be known for? Phil was considering carefully, remembering that he had only two guesses left, when his mother's voice put an end to his efforts.

"Game's off, Phil." She had put on her bonnet, he noted, and was making a neat bow of its ribbons. "Your sister, too, has no knowledge of the great celebration that's to be. I'll tell you both about it as we walk to church. Are you ready, Mary?"

"Yes, Mama." Mary, too, was putting on her bonnet.

"Good." With which Mrs. Sheridan, prayer book in hand, marched to the door—but no farther. "Whisht!" She whirled around. "It's the great forgetfulness that will be my undoing yet. The rosary, Phil. You will find it there by the flatirons on the fireplace mantel. Fetch it, please, and we'll be on our way."

★ ★ ★ ★ ★ ★ ★ ★ ★ ★ ★ ★ ★ ★

2

The Indian Fighter

The morning was cool but there was a heavy, clinging feel to the air that promised a hot day later on. The church was half a mile away. Their route lay partly through the orchard, partly across a field behind the house where the Greiners lived, partly up a long hill, abloom at this season with Jimson weed and the gaudy blossoms of the pinkster flower.

Any other day Phil would have been charging restlessly ahead, stopping at some such point of interest as the creek to wait for the more leisurely womenfolk to catch up. Today he stuck close to his mother.

Her statement that there was to be a celebration had not been wasted on his sister's ears. Mary was the first to speak as the three of them crossed the back yard and strolled northward along the orchard path.

"Did I understand you correctly, Mama? There's to be some sort of celebration?"

"Aye, Mary. Celebration was my very word."

"Today?"

"Today's the day, and twelve o'clock noon the hour, if all goes as planned. Our boy here, no doubt, will be going to town with his pal Hank. But you and I, once our chores are done, will put on our best clothes and go together."

Phil caught a touch of laughter in his mother's voice. He sighed. He knew what it meant. Mama would talk all around the subject practically the whole way to church. She would amuse herself by keeping him and Mary guessing for as long as possible.

"Well?" said Mary.

"Well," said Mrs. Sheridan.

They were walking along the western fringe of the orchard. To their left the land sloped toward the dense woods of the Hocking River valley. Mrs. Sheridan made a fan of her prayer book and said, "Don't the two of you feel the heat that is soon to be upon us?"

Phil sought his sister's eyes. Mary's lifted brows told him that, like himself, she was on to what was happening.

"About the celebration, Mama?" Mary asked.

"Ah, yes." Mrs. Sheridan fanned vigorously. "As I was saying to your brother before you honored us with your presence in the kitchen, Mrs. Ritchie came by last evening late. Her husband was in Baltimore and came home yesterday with the news." She paused.

Phil ran a hand through his mother's arm. "What news?" he urged.

"I've already told you. There's to be a celebration. A grand and glorious celebration with all the trimmings." A smile overspread Mrs. Sheridan's features as she thought about the pleasant prospect.

"The celebration," Mary reminded her mother, laughing in spite of herself. "What's it for?"

"A distinguished visitor. Our guest of honor, arriving on the twelve o'clock stage from the East, will be none other than the Vice President of the United States of America!"

There was no further conversation for the time being. Mary was pleased. Whether it was because she was going to set eyes on a vice president or because they were having an unexpected holiday would be hard to say. But pleased she was, as witness the smiles wreathing her dimpled face.

Phil was conscious of a faint feeling of letdown. Since the visitor wasn't a general, he had rather hoped he would be some sort of military man or at the very least a canal builder.

His face registered his disappointment, or rather his eyes did. Brown ordinarily, his eyes had a way of changing color as his feelings changed, sometimes becoming almost black, again almost red. He was a small boy for his age, and his proportions were downright funny. His arms were unusually long, his legs unusually short. Most of his fights were with boys who called him a monkey. He fought for other reasons, to be sure; and sometimes for no reason at all. He didn't always win, but it was never for lack of trying. Behind the little fellow's narrow, slanted eyes was something very big indeed—a temper. It was a trigger temper at that. When aroused, he became a raging, writhing, hard-fisted bundle of fury.

His mother was gazing at him. "Disappointed?" she inquired.

"Oh, no. I mean, not really. I mean . . ." Phil couldn't lie. He reddened and subsided into silence.

They had reached the creek. It was a mad little stream. Its rock-strewn waters brought memories to the boy, memories of trout whisked from its depths, of suckers speared from its sandbars.

His mother rolled out a low chuckle. "Be of good cheer," she told him. "I have something to add that will make you feel better. The Vice President is also a colonel."

"A fighting man?"

"He fought in the War of 1812. Some say 'twas he who killed Tecumseh." Wrinkles gathered in Phil's forehead, and his mother was quick to notice them. "Doesn't that name mean anything to you?" she asked.

"I dunno. I know a Tecumseh—I mean I've talked with him. Only folks call him Cump for short. Cump Sherman's his name. Mary knows him. He lives in Lancaster and he goes to West Point and he's got a girl. Her name's . . . her name's . . ."

His sister helped him out. "Phil's talking about Ellen Ewing, Mama. She goes to school with me."

At this point the school of which Mary was speaking, St. Mary's Female Academy, was within view. A rambling wooden building, it stood on the crest of Academy Hill, next door to St. Mary's Church and the small red-brick house occupied by the priest-brothers, Father Joshua and Father Dominic Young.

Mrs. Sheridan was nodding and saying, "Ah, yes, ah, yes." She enlightened her son. "You're talking about William Tecumseh Sherman," she informed him. "Cadet Sherman, if you're of a mind to be fussy about it. He lives with Senator Ewing and his wife in Lancaster and goes with their daughter Ellen."

They were leaving the orchard for the open field. Here

there was no protection from the rising sun, and Mrs. Sheridan treated herself to another fanning with her prayer book. "I," she said, "am speaking of quite a different person. The Tecumseh to whom I refer was a great Indian chief. He was chief of the Shawnee tribe. A sort of emperor he was, too, ruling over many tribes. A very great man, probably the greatest of all the Indian chiefs."

Phil's eyes, alight with interest, never left his mother's face as she continued: "During the War of 1812," she related, "Tecumseh got mad at the Americans. He had good reasons, which I forget. Anyhow, he fought on the side of the British. And this man who is coming to us today—our present Vice President—he is the man who slew the great Tecumseh *in single-handed combat.*"

Mrs. Sheridan put great emphasis on her final words, and each of them went like an arrow straight to the boy's heart.

"An Indian fighter," he murmured in awed tones. "An Indian fighter!" A sudden thought, a great possibility seized him. "Tell me something, Mama. When the Indian fighter gets here—the Vice President, I mean—is there going to be handshaking?"

"I fancy the great man will shake hands with the grownups."

"But not with us boys?"

"If there's time perhaps and under certain circumstances."

"Circumstances? What kind of circumstances?"

"Oh, I don't think the Vice President would object to shaking hands with a boy with a clean face and clean hands, not to mention a decent pair of overalls on his person."

"I'll scrub, Mama. And I'll change clothes. But I'm telling you something right now." Phil grabbed his mother's arm to make certain of her attention. "If the Indian fighter shakes

13

hands with me, I won't wash my right hand. I won't wash it for a whole week. I swear it. You can whip me dead, and I won't wash it."

Mrs. Sheridan laughed, then suddenly sobered. "Philip!" The sharpness of her tone made the boy hop. "What is the name of the Vice President of the United States?"

"You mean the Indian fighter?"

"And who else would I be speaking of, seeing as the Indian fighter and the Vice President are one and the same man. What is his name?"

"Why, it's . . . Why . . . a . . . Mr. Martin Van Buren, he's President."

"That I'll not deny. But what is the name of his Vice President?"

"Why. . . a . . Ah, Mama, I don't know."

Mrs. Sheridan pursed her lips. "In that case," she said severely, "I'll be after asking you another question. Where were you, Philip, a week ago last Monday?"

"A week ago last Monday." Phil gulped. "I was ... I was . . . Why do you want to know, Mama?"

"I'll tell you why. A week ago last Monday Mr. McManly, your esteemed schoolmaster, gave a special lesson in history. During the course of that lesson he told his students the names of all the high officials of the United States Government, including the President— and the Vice President!"

They had reached the lower slope of Academy Hill. As they began the ascent, Mrs. Sheridan gave a slight hitch to her long, full skirt and its numerous petticoats. "I take it," she resumed, "that you are now beginning to get the gist and point of my remarks. You don't know the name of the Vice President because a week ago last Monday, instead of being in school where you belonged, you were playing hooky with your great friend and companion-in-crime, Hank Greiner!"

Phil stopped dead in his tracks. Again he had to skip to catch up. Who? Who could have snitched on him? He himself had told nobody but his sister. Mary was looking his way now. He shot her an accusing glance.

She shook her head. "No, Phil. I didn't say a word. Did I, Mama?"

Mrs. Sheridan shook hers. "No." She gave her attention once more to Phil. "There's something that I do not think you quite realize. Your father and I and Mr. McManly, your esteemed schoolmaster, all knew each other very well in the old country. Before leaving town for the summer Mr. McManly paid me a call."

The hill was getting steeper. Mrs. Sheridan gave her prayer book a few flaps. "We had a cozy cup of tea together," she went on. "In the kitchen this was, and Mr. McManly was kind enough to give me a report on your activities during the school year. Ah, what a mournful tale it was: the countless times you played hooky; the morning you and Hank put that water above the schoolhouse door, drenching Mr. McManly to the skin so that the poor man caught his death of cold. Not to mention your fights in the schoolhouse yard."

"Fights? Me?"

"Yes, you! Don't misunderstand me. Every boy is privileged to have a few fights. Alas, how you abuse the privilege!"

"I can't help myself, Mama. I'm little and the boys make fun of me and . . ."

"Silence, child!" Mrs. Sheridan enforced her order with a quick rap of her knuckles on the boy's head. "What difference does it make whether your body is long or short? Bigness has nothing to do with what you look like on the outside. Bigness has to do with what you *are* on the inside. Do you ken the

The water poured down on Mr. McManly.

meaning of that statement?"

Phil didn't but he said he did.

His mother was not taken in. "Never mind," she said, "you will in due time. When you do understand, my boy, then you'll be a man—a great, grand man like your father."

Mrs. Sheridan paused to take in air. "No," she went on shortly, "you don't have too many fights because you're small. You have too many fights because your temper is so big."

"Me, Mama? Temper?"

"Yes, Phil, you, temper! And that brings me to another question: what do you plan on being when it's grown up you are?"

"You know that. A soldier."

"What kind?"

"A general. What else?"

"Don't generals fight battles, and don't they fight to win—to get victories?"

"Naturally."

"Very well then. You listen to this, my fine young bucko, and listen well. Before you win any victories over anyone else, you're going to have to win a little victory over yourself. You're going to have to learn how to control that temper."

Mrs. Sheridan punctuated this statement with a sharp nod of her head. On they trudged in what for a few minutes was a painful silence. Then, "Mama," Phil ventured, "what is the name of the Vice President?"

The sternness ebbed from Mrs. Sheridan's eyes. She smiled. "Johnson," she said. "Colonel Richard Mentor Johnson of Kentucky. Now what is the name?"

Phil said it. "Colonel Something Johnson."

"Richard Mentor Johnson. Of where?"

"Kentucky."

"Correct." Mrs. Sheridan's smile broadened. "And there's things you should know about him, the fine, good things he's done."

"Such as?" from Phil.

"Such as being a member of the United States Senate and of the House of Representatives, not to mention Governor of his state. Wounded he was in the Battle of the Thames on the Canadian border in the War of 1812. It was the Americans against the British, and the Americans carried the day, thanks to our colonel. Himself was borne from the field, a great hero."

"And does he have medals?" Phil could not forbear from asking.

"Medals is it! It's a crippled hand he has. And that's medal enough for any man as has the satisfaction of knowing that he has served his country well."

As she ceased speaking, Mrs. Sheridan halted and looked up the hill, shading her eyes with a hand. Some fifty feet beyond stood two men in the white robes of the Dominican Order.

"Ah," Mrs. Sheridan murmured in a voice as soft as a caress. "If it isn't the good Fathers themselves. Sure and they look like twins astanding there."

At this distance the priest-brothers did look alike. But close up, as Phil knew, they were different in every way. Father Joshua, the older and taller, was heavy and severe in his manner. It was quite otherwise with Father Dominic, a free and easy man, full of fun and jokes. It was his cheery voice that came down the hill to them as they resumed their climb.

"A good morning to you, Mrs. Sheridan," he called. "And to you, Miss Mary, and Philip."

"And a very good day to you, Fathers," Mrs. Sheridan called back.

Phil smiled and waved. His mother's stern words were forgotten for the moment. He was thinking of the great man who would be coming to town on the noon stage, of Vice President Richard Mentor Johnson, military hero and Indian fighter. A very good day it was, he was thinking. And, of course, the best was yet to come.

★ ★ ★ ★ ★ ★ ★ ★ ★ ★ ★ ★ ★ ★

3

THE WHIG BOY

Little Phil went at his chores with unusual vigor that morning. In short order the kitchen woodbox was filled, the horse fed and the eggs gathered.

At the last moment his mother put the wash-tub in his room, filled it with hot water and ordered him to take a bath. This outrage was submitted to promptly, if not enthusiastically, with the result that by midmorning Phil was racing through the orchard en route to the Greiner home.

There he was informed that his pal Hank had already gone to town. Even as this knowledge was being imparted, Hank's mother was pouring milk from a pitcher and putting cookies on a plate. Politeness forbade him from leaving until these items had been consumed. There was a further delay while he and Mrs. Greiner exchanged a few remarks dealing with the weather (very hot now) and with the impending festivities in honor of the visit of Vice President Richard Mentor Johnson. Once more on his way, Phil made a beeline for the center of town, two blocks distant.

Main Street, running due east and west, was part of the Kentucky turnpike, one of the highways his father had helped to build. Its landmarks were the county courthouse on the square at the western end, the hotel known as Finch's Tavern toward the east and its neighboring livery stable where the stagecoach bringing the Vice President would pause long enough for its four sweating horses to be relieved and fresh ones put into their traces.

Crossing the turnpike at the halfway point was Columbus Street, a stony lane that divided the town itself into two sections. The western half where the Sheridans lived overlooked the valley of the Hocking and was known as Pig Foot. The eastern half, overlooking the Muskingum River valley, was called Turkey Trot. An unspoken law of the town was that a Pig Foot boy and a Turkey Trot boy, meeting for the first time, must have a fight, after which it was not uncommon for the two of them to become friends for life.

The bustle that met Phil's eyes as he emerged from the alley that had brought him to town was all that he had hoped it would be. Obviously the news had made its way far into the countryside. The farmers were streaming in. Already the teams that pulled the buggies and buckboard wagons were shoulder to shoulder along the tie rails in front of the low, wooden buildings with their white fronts and overhanging eaves. Small boys were all over the place, chasing in and out among the parked vehicles, or sparring with one another, or rolling in friendly wrestles in the dusty roadbed.

The crowd was thickest in the vicinity of Finch's Tavern.

Dodging and sidestepping his way through, Phil caught a glimpse of his mother and sister. They were on the porch of Finck and Dittoe's Dry Goods Store directly across from the tavern.

He shouted at them, but to no avail. His voice was powerless against the surrounding din. Besides, as he could see, Mama and Mary were having the time of their lives, laughing and trading gossip with the other ladies on the porch.

Everywhere he turned he saw familiar faces. Stopping for conversation with one person and then another, he quickly got a line on the order of events. A committee of prominent citizens, already assembled on the tavern porch, was to welcome the Vice President. Then he was to be escorted inside for his dinner. Next on the schedule would be his speech from the balcony. Last of all would come the handshaking. This event, Phil learned, would take place in the tavern lobby, or, as it was usually and more accurately called, the barroom.

Searching for Hank, he first tried the livery stable. He hustled in and out of half-a-dozen other places before he caught sight of his friend, horseplaying around with a gang of boys in front of the blacksmith's shop.

Hank was a year his senior, and a good half a head taller, a lanky lad with a square and densely freckled face. Seeing Phil, even before Phil's voice had reached him through the racket, he grinned like a jack-o'-lantern and came running.

The pals greeted one another in their usual manner, which is to say with a good deal of weaving this way and that, and a great show of fisticuffs.

"Thought some of dropping by for you," was Hank's opening gambit, circling rapidly to his right as he spoke and jabbing good-naturedly at Phil. "Only I figured you'd be long gone."

"Held up at the last minute. Had to take a bath."

"Heck you did!" from Hank, dancing now to his left.

"Heck I didn't," from Phil, dancing to his right. "Know what Mama says? She says maybe he'll shake hands with us boys."

"He will? Who will?"

"The Colonel. Who else? You know who he is, don't you?"

"Know who he is! Sure I know. He's the man who killed Tecumseh."

"And that isn't all!" cried Phil, eager to show off the knowledge so recently acquired from his mother. "He's Vice President, too. Vice President of the United States of America!"

"And *that* isn't all!" Hank came back at him like a bounced ball. "He isn't only the Vice President this very minute. Maybe he will be again. The Democrats have just nominated him to run on the ticket with President Van Buren for another four-year term."

"The Dem . . . ! The Demo . . . !"

No more circling on Phil's part.

His eyes, his whole face turned color and his throat gagged over the word.

Closing in on his pal, fists still at the ready, he stared him straight in the eye. "Hank Greiner!" he cried. "Are you going to stand there and tell me that Colonel Richard Mentor Johnson, the Indian fighter, is a . . . is a . . ." There was only one way to get the horrid word into the open. He spit it out. "Is a *Democrat!*"

Uncertain what to expect next, Hank also came to a halt. He threw one leg back for better fighting stance, just in case. "Of course he's a Democrat," he retorted. "Everybody knows that."

"Everybody?"

"Everybody!"

"Oh!" Phil's hands fell, and then his head.

He was stunned, shaken.

Somehow, listening to his mother that morning, it hadn't occurred to him to check on the Colonel's politics. But now that he thought about it, of course the Colonel was a Democrat. President Van Buren was, and in next fall's presidential election it was going to be Van Buren of New York and Johnson *versus* William Henry Harrison of Ohio and John Tyler of Virginia.

Phil sighed. It was one of those sighs that begins deep and takes its time getting out. Phil was a little weak on history, but he was up on his politics. His father had seen to that. The Republican Party had not yet been organized, nor would it be for almost another decade and a half. The great political parties of the day were the Democrats and the Whigs.

And Phil was a Whig! That is, his mother and father were Whigs. Had anyone asked Phil just what the Whigs stood for, he would have been hard put to say. But as for the Democrats! He had his father's word for it. They were the errand boys of the devil himself!

Just then into the glum silence came a familiar sound—a plaintive, lingering, rising-and-falling sound—the sound of the stage-coach-driver's horn as he drove his horses down Harper's Hill some distance out of town for the last lap of his journey into Somerset. A second time the blast came, and before the last echo had faded, the cannon on Reading Hill began booming at a rapid rate.

The earth shook around Phil as everybody who wasn't already in the neighborhood of the tavern proceeded to get there as fast as his legs could carry him. The boys Hank had been playing with ran by shouting.

As for Hank himself, he remained where he was, gazing in

a bewildered manner at the lowered head of his pal. "Come on, Phil," he urged. "Come on. That's the stage, that's him!" Then again, having received no reply. "I said that's the stage, Phil. Come on!"

Phil's eyes were still on the ground. "I'm not going," he said.

"Not going! You mean you're gonna pass up a chance to shake hands with an Indian fighter!"

"I'm not shaking hands with any Democrats."

"Oh, so that's it."

"Yes, that's it."

Whereupon Phil turned on his heel and moved off, away from the tavern.

Had he looked back he would have seen his friend start to follow, then stop. Finally, with a shrug, Hank turned on his own heel and skedaddled in the direction of the crowd gathering around the tavern porch.

But Phil didn't look back. He kept going, walking slowly at first, and then faster, and at length running.

He turned down the alley past the long wagon shed that was part of the blacksmith's establishment. When he had cleared the shed, he left the alley and struck out diagonally across an open lot. It was a big, weedy lot, broken here and there by sandy hillocks. When he ran out of breath, he made for one of the hillocks and threw himself down, resting his back against it.

He shut his eyes and got his breath and thought.

He wished with all his heart that he'd asked his mother about Colonel Johnson's politics. He wished she were right here with him now. More to the point, he wished his father were. His father would tell him; he would know whether or not he was doing the right thing.

But, no, he quickly told himself. No! He didn't need his father to tell him. Of course he was doing the right thing. Whigs were Whigs and Democrats were Democrats, and what kind of world would it be if Whigs went around shaking hands with Democrats all over the place!

There was the cannon booming again, and then the stagecoach horn, so close that it made the windows jump in the rear of the blacksmith's shop. Phil could hear the people shouting over yonder on the far side of the buildings.

It was the shouting that nearly did him in. It came to him suddenly, sickeningly, that he was going to cry!

Right then and there he resolved that he wouldn't let himself do so. He wouldn't if it killed him not to. He gritted his teeth so hard that they ached. It was a trick that he'd used before. It had always worked.

It worked this time. When he realized that the spell had passed, that he didn't feel like crying any longer, he released his teeth, feeling as exhausted as if he'd just walked a hundred and fifty miles.

He scooched his back into the sand of the little hill and listened hard. No sound was coming from Main Street now—that is, no shouts or anything unusual. He knew what that meant. The Vice President was eating his dinner. There would be cheering again when he came out to speak.

There it was now. And what cheers they were: wave on wave of them in a soaring surge of sound! Shortly he realized that the people were chanting something. Pretty soon he caught the words:

Rumpsey, dumpsey!
Colonel Johnson
Killed Tecumseh!

The crowd gathered as the stagecoach pulled up.

Over and over, the chant was repeated, in swelling waves of sound.

He put his palms to his ears and didn't take them away until the chanting ceased.

He got to his feet. Better go someplace, find something to do. No point just sitting here, driving himself crazy, thinking about all the wonderful things that were going on over there and that he was missing.

He walked fast. When he reached the alley again, he stopped. He had the funny feeling that somebody was staring at him. But who, he wondered, looking all around. Presently he discovered who it was.

At this point there was a picket fence along the alley with a yard behind it and at the end of the yard a small, neat cottage. There was an old woman sitting on the cottage porch. She

was sitting in a chair known as a jiggle chair. It was a straight chair with its front legs cushioned in coil springs. There the old lady sat, jiggling contentedly and puffing on a corncob pipe.

Phil knew the old lady well. It was Mrs. Harper, who, he realized, wasn't really seeing him. With her weak old eyes, she couldn't make out a small boy ten feet away. But the old lady could hear. She leaned forward suddenly. Removing the pipe from her mouth, she turned her head one way and then the other. It came to Phil that the good old woman was trying to "see," so to speak, with her ears.

He called to her. "It's me, Mrs. Harper. Phil Sheridan."

"Phil Sheridan!" Her voice cracked but it was still full of life. "Phil Sheridan," the old lady said again. "Now let me see. That would be John and Mary Sheridan's oldest child."

"No, Mrs. Harper. There's two older than me and three younger."

"Ah, yes, ah, yes. But here, here, boy!" The old lady bent forward again. "Why aren't you at the big celebration over there at Finch's Tavern?"

Why indeed! Phil sighed. Noticing a pebble on the ground, he lifted it between the toes of his right foot. With a kicking movement of his leg, he spun it into the air. "It's like this, Mrs. Harper," he said. "Colonel Johnson's a Democrat and I'm a Whig boy."

"I declare," said the old lady. "I do declare." She returned her pipe to her mouth, puffed briefly and removed it again. It was a strong pipe, Phil decided, as a slight shift of the wind brought him a sample of its fragrance.

The old lady's mouth made some little movements as if she were rehearsing her next remark. She broke into speech in due time. "A Whig boy, eh?" she murmured. "And what's more a boy who has the courage to act on his convictions. That speaks well for you, Phil Sheridan, but—"

The old lady jabbed at the air with the stem of her pipe. "But," she said with more force than before, "would it be against your principles now just to go and have a look at what's happening? You wouldn't have to clap your hands when the great man spoke. You wouldn't have to join in the cheering. But surely, boy, there'd be no harm in just looking. After all, you're only young once, and it's a pity to be shut out of all the fun."

Mrs. Harper leaned back in her chair, puffed again, spoke again. "Am I not right?" she inquired pertly. "Would it be untrue to your principles now, just to go and have a peek, boy?"

Phil was thinking. He fastened his eyes on the pebble he

had just sent flying to the side of the alley and thought very hard. Mrs. Harper's suggestion put a new light on things—yes, quite a new light; in fact, a dazzling light.

The voice of the old lady, speaking once more, had a wheedling, coaxing quality. "How about it, Phil boy? Why don't you run on now and have yourself a little look?"

"I reckon there's something in what you say, Mrs. Harper. Yes, there's a lot in it. I'll do it. Good day to you, ma'am!"

He was off. He ran the whole way. Never had his feet carried him with less effort. Never had his heart been lighter.

A rousing cheer was arising from the crowd as he emerged from the alley into Main Street. A quick glance toward the tavern told him what was happening. Colonel Johnson had finished speaking and was leaving the balcony. Down below, the people were moving into the tavern barroom.

By the time Phil reached the tavern, not a person remained outside. Through the open front door he could see a dense crowd within. There were times when being small had its advantages and this was one of them. Squeezing his way he wedged himself rapidly forward.

Busy getting where he was going, he didn't notice his friend Hank, standing with a gang of boys over near the hotel desk. Had he noticed he might have been amused at the startled expression on his friend's face, at the way Hank's jack-o'-lantern grin took form and slowly widened until it nearly reached his ears on either side.

Phil, of course, had no eyes for Hank. Having arrived at the forefront of the crowd, he fixed his whole attention on the scene before him.

He had trouble making out Colonel Johnson's features. The Vice President was standing at the rear of the room in the shadows of a shallow alcove. Grouped about him were the members of the welcoming committee, headed by a local general, himself a veteran of the War of 1812. Phil, trying to make out the Colonel's appearance, got the impression of a medium-sized man who held himself in a soldierly manner and whose hair was graying; nothing more.

The Colonel was shaking hands with the grownups. The people moved past him in an orderly line. The Colonel nodded to each of them and said something—something that Phil couldn't hear because the room was full of boys and practically every one of them was carrying on a muttered conversation with the others around him.

As each of the grownups finished shaking hands, he crossed the room and left the tavern by a side door leading into the alley. It was all over in no time. The Colonel turned and talked in low tones to the members of the welcoming committee. Phil could see the general in charge nodding.

Then, turning back, the Colonel moved into the room a few steps. Holding up his hand he commanded—and got—silence.

"All right, boys," he said. "I understand my stage won't be leaving for another ten minutes. I've had the pleasure of meeting your parents. Now I should very much like to have the privilege of shaking your hands, if you don't mind."

There was an instant rush in the direction of the alcove. Phil was caught off guard. He hadn't thought to consider what he should do when this happened. Of course there was only one thing to do. Somehow he must push either to the front door or the side door and get away.

Easier said than done! Wedging through a crowd of grownups, as he just had, was one thing. Bucking a rushing, screaming crowd of boys was something else. He was caught like a stone in a slingshot and hurled toward the Colonel.

Before he could collect his thoughts, he was standing smack in front of the Vice President of the United States, his head lifted and his eyes on the famed Indian fighter's face.

It was his first close look, and it gave him the shock of his life. Phil knew a good face when he saw one, and Democrat or no Democrat, the Vice President had a good face! You couldn't call it handsome exactly, but it was strong and the features were clear cut. Phil was reminded of pictures of ancient Greek warriors he had once seen in a book that Mr. McManly had handed around at school.

It was a terrible moment for him, terrible and bewildering. And it was followed by one that was even worse. The Colonel extended his hand. And when Phil saw it, he wished the floor would open and let him drop from sight.

It was a crippled hand! Through his mind flashed the things his mother had told him that morning: How Colonel Johnson had fought at the Battle of the Thames, how he had battled with Tecumseh, how he had been wounded and borne, a hero, from the field!

And now the hand—the hand that had been wounded— was being offered to him and he couldn't take it!

He flung his own hands behind him and hung his head. The silence the Colonel had commanded was already a thing of the past. Phil could hear gasps from the other boys, then murmurs, then voices.

"What's the matter, Phil! Ain't your pappy taught you how to shake hands!"

"What's the matter, Phil! Too short to reach that high?"

And hardest of all to bear, first from one throat and then from several in a chorus: "Monkey! Monkey! Monkey!"

Then silence, sudden and complete.

Looking up, Phil saw why. The Vice President had lifted

his crippled hand. "That'll be enough, boys," he said quietly. "That'll be enough."

He bent his face to Phil.

"Little boy," he said, "won't you shake hands with me?"

"No, sir. I don't want to."

"Why not?"

"Because I'm a Whig."

"Oh, that makes no difference."

"Yes, sir. It does. It isn't right."

The Vice President smiled. He raised his head and looked around, speaking quietly as before. "Boys," he said, "give way and let this little Whig out. We can't force or coax him to shake hands with a Democrat."

The boys made a lane for Phil to the front door. He scooted across the porch, down the steps. He wasn't conscious of running in any particular direction. He was surprised, pounding across South Street, to find himself at home.

He kept running until, at the far end of the back yard, he arrived at what he and Hank called their "Secret Place."

Actually it was a willow. What made it secret was the great size of the tree. It was an ancient tree. On all sides its delicate limbs fell clean to the ground so that when the tree was in full leaf its greenery dropped a thick curtain around an area some twelve to fifteen feet in diameter.

Crashing through the overhanging limbs, Phil threw himself onto the soft ground of the dark area within. Now the tears came, the tears he'd been holding back. They kept coming no matter how hard he gritted his teeth. They kept coming until every tear that had been in him was out.

★ ★ ★ ★ ★ ★ ★ ★ ★ ★ ★ ★ ★ ★

4

A Tough Problem

In later years Phil Sheridan sometimes recalled, with a chuckle, how he refused to take the hand of the Vice President of the United States because the Vice President was a Democrat and he a Whig. Naturally, as time went on, he realized that he had been wrong. What political party a man belonged to didn't make all that difference.

Learning this was part of his growing up. And Phil grew up fast. He had to. He had no choice in the matter.

He was still a boy when his father got into financial difficulties. A contracting job, undertaken by Mr. Sheridan, required longer to complete than he had expected it would. Instead of making money on the job, he lost money, a misfortune that made a change in his son's life. In his fourteenth year Phil had to leave school to help support his family while his father tried to recover from his losses.

Phil worked in a general store.

He worked for one year in John Talbot's hardware and grocery store. Mr. Talbot was a silent man with a face like a frosty night. He never smiled and he kept his clerks hopping. Phil dealt out coffee and spices and bolts and nuts. His work was hard, his hours long, his salary—two dollars a month.

He did very well, much to his mother's amazement. "It's the proud surprise you are to me, Phil," she told him as one Sunday afternoon they shared a cup of tea together at the kitchen table. "A proud and happy surprise," she continued in her musical way. "I've heard it said that you are the politest clerk in town, and such words are a joy to your old mother's heart. Keep it up, boy. Keep it up."

Phil kept it up. The next year found him making more money at another store and the next found him at Finck and Dittoe's Dry Goods Store, working as bookkeeper with a salary of ten dollars a month.

Like most small-town dry goods stores of the period, Finck and Dittoe's was really a general store. Dangling on wires from its rafters were men's vests and baskets, hatboxes and carpetbags, hoopskirts and parrot cages. Bolts of patterned cotton, calico, crockery, glassware, spices, molasses and indigo crowded its pine shelves. Horsewhips stood in earthenware jugs in the corners. On the wooden counters could be found coffee grinders and candles, mechanical wooden apple-peelers and gift items.

Phil worked behind a high counter in the rear. Right in front of him, in a clearing, was the heart of the store. Here stood the potbellied stove, the cracker barrel, some benches and some chairs. And here, on winter days, the customers gathered to talk over current events.

During Phil's first months at Finck and Dittoed, much of the talk revolved about a local controversy. The subject of the controversy was the new schoolmaster, or more exactly the new schoolmaster's ideas.

Mr. McManly, the "esteemed schoolmaster" of Phil's childhood, had long since left town. His successor, a Mr. Thorne, had been a man of similar stripe. Like Mr. McManly before him, Mr. Thorne believed that the only way to get anything into a boy's head was to pound it in by laying a hickory stick athwart the seat of his breeches.

The new schoolmaster, taking over only a few months before, thought otherwise. His name was William Clark. He hailed from what the people of Somerset called "Back East," and was often spoken of as the Connecticut Yankee.

Mr. Clark did not whip his students. He taught them. The townspeople had no serious objections to this. In fact it was soon plain to most of them that the children were learning more and faster under the Connecticut Yankee without benefit of hickory stick than had ever been the case under McManly and Thorne with their endless whippings.

The excitement began when the news spread that Mr. Clark had put up a blackboard at the front of the Somerset schoolhouse. Some people thought this was going a bit far, and by the next morning the whole town was talking of little else. Within a week there were arguments and wrangles between two groups of almost equal size, an Anti-Blackboard group and a Pro-Blackboard group.

Finally Mr. Clark, the Connecticut Yankee teacher, persuaded the townspeople to hold a meeting at the schoolhouse and end the argument by taking a vote. If a majority favored getting rid of the blackboard, it was to go; if not, it was to stay.

The meeting lasted far into the night. The Anti-Blackboard people defended their position in a string of explosive orations. Their chief argument was that if the blackboard stayed, the children of Somerset would never learn anything. They would spend all their time in school "drawin' pitchers."

When the Pro-Blackboard people got their turn, they orated even longer and louder. "It is time Somerset enjoyed some progress," declared a Pro-Blackboard man. "After all, we're not living in the Middle Ages any more. This is 1847. We folks ought to start doing things the way they're done in the big cities like New York and Philadelphia."

On and on the arguments went. At a late hour, mostly because people had become too tired to talk any more, the vote was taken. The Pro-Blackboard forces won by a small margin, and the people of Somerset turned their minds to other matters.

There were plenty for them to turn to. America was at war with Mexico. Phil was too young to enlist, but he wasn't too young to read the newspapers, and what he read stayed with him. He had a good mind for campaigns and battles. It wasn't long before people were dropping into Finck and Dittoe's to get young Sheridan's opinion of this or that military maneuver down in Mexico.

Phil had by no means given up his childhood ambition to be a soldier. He was very busy now, and as bookkeeper for Finck and Dittoe's his responsibilities were heavy for a seventeen-year-old youth. There wasn't much time to think of other matters. But every now and then, walking home from work or during a slow spell in the shop, he would dream his old dreams. He would say to himself, "One of these days, one of these days, my chance will come."

It came sooner than he or anyone else had expected. In Phil's day a boy could not get into the United States Military Academy at West Point, New York, by taking a competitive examination. He had to be appointed by the man who represented his Congressional District in the lower house of the United States Congress. As a rule, the name of the candidate appointed in each district was made public in February or March. The following summer the candidate enrolled at West Point. There, toward the end of his first month, he took his examinations for admission. If he passed, he stayed; if not, he went home.

In 1847 the candidate named in Phil's Congressional District had had to return home. The minute Phil heard about this he got busy. He wrote a letter to his Congressman in Washington. He asked to be appointed to the Academy in place of the boy who had failed to pass his examinations for admission.

Quite likely Phil smiled to himself as the letter was being written, for the Congressman to whom he was sending this heartfelt request was his old friend and neighbor, Thomas Ritchie—and it will be recalled that Mr. Ritchie was a Democrat.

Phil knew anxious days as he waited for Congressman Ritchie's reply. He was at his desk at the rear of Finck and Dittoe's when it came, an impressive-looking envelope with the printed words "U. S. House of Representatives" in the upper left-hand corner.

With trembling hands Phil opened the letter. Pulling out the sheet of paper within, he laid it on his desk. He read it once, twice. He told himself that he must be reading the words wrong, that what he was reading just couldn't be true.

But it was! The paper was his appointment. It ordered him to report to West Point on or before June 1, 1848.

Phil read the document a third time. "Eureka!" he shouted.

He said it so loudly that Mr. Henry Dittoe, his boss, came

running back from the front of the store. Mr. Dittoe was a tall man with an angular, pleasant face. He knew that Phil had written his Congressman. And when he heard Phil's shout he knew that he had received his answer.

"Your appointment?" he inquired.

Phil indicated the sheet of paper on his desk.

"Congratulations," said Mr. Dittoe.

Phil took the hand his boss extended, but he was frowning. "Not so fast," he said. "I may never get there."

"But of course you'll get there."

"I'm not so sure. We've been having some arguments about it."

"We?"

"My father and I."

Mr. Dittoe's eyebrows lifted slightly. "Doesn't your father want you to go to West Point?"

"He's anything but pleased at the idea."

"Why not?"

Phil's smile was not a bright one. "Papa has his reasons," he said. His eyes, drifting across the store, came to rest on the grandfather's clock standing between two of the windows. "Look, Mr. Dittoe, my father's at home today and I think the sooner I talk with him the better. Could I have your kind permission to take the rest of the afternoon off?"

"But, of course, of course."

Phil removed the paper cuffs he wore to keep his shirt clean while he worked. He put on his long jacket and stuffed Mr. Ritchie's letter into one of the pockets.

Phil was the possessor now of a thick black mustache. Otherwise he had not changed a great deal. He had lengthened out some, but not much. He was still short for his age. He still had long arms and short legs and a bullet head, so shaped that he had trouble finding hats to fit it.

He walked home rapidly. Somerset was having one of those August days so common to the Midwest—when the sun, sheeting the open fields, is deep yellow in color, when there is no movement of any sort in the air and every growing thing within range of the eye takes on a still and waiting look.

Mrs. Sheridan was in the back yard, hanging out the washing. She saw her son before he saw her, and glanced anxiously at the sky. "Is it sick you are," she called to him, "that you're home in the middle of the afternoon?"

"No, Mama. I'm not sick. It's this."

Phil handed her the appointment.

Mrs. Sheridan, having read it, looked toward the house. "The others are gone," she said significantly. "Your father's alone."

Mr. Sheridan was sitting at the kitchen table, studying some maps spread out before him. He was a stocky, strong-looking man, slow in movement and speech. He had worked hard all his life and he had known no small amount of trouble. Fatigue and worry had drawn ridgelike lines about his eyes and mouth.

He looked up as his son entered. He nodded.

Phil dropped his appointment on the table. "It's come, Papa," he said.

Mr. Sheridan scanned the document and handed it back in silence. Briefly the fingers of one of his heavy hands drummed the table. Then rising and getting his hat from a peg on the wall, "Come," he said, going toward the door.

"But where are we off to?"

"Up the hill, son. This thing must be settled now, and there's only two men who can tell us what to do. And that's the priest-brothers, Father Joshua and Father Dominic."

Mrs. Sheridan was out of sight, filling the clotheslines over beyond the chicken coop, as father and son emerged from the house. No words passed between them as they walked through the orchard, across the field behind the Greiners' and up the long, lazily rising hill.

Locust trees shaded the little brick house where the priests lived. The housekeeper, opening the door to them, disappeared for a moment and returned, saying both priests were in and would see them in the living room.

The living room was small, and its worn furnishings, heavy pieces all of them, gave it a crowded and hemmed-in look.

Father Joshua had been writing at the table under the side window. He rose as Mr. Sheridan and Phil entered. Father Dominic, already on his feet, put aside the book from which he had been reading the Office and hurried over to shake their hands. He was a chunky young man with a round, beaming face. His older brother, on the other hand, had a long face and solemn half-moon eyes. He too shook hands and motioned his visitors to chairs as he returned to his own.

For a few minutes the conversation was general, mostly about the weather which all present agreed was uncomfortable. Then Mr. Sheridan broached the problem that had brought him and Phil to the priests' house.

His first words were to Father Joshua. "It is about the matter you and I were discussing the other day."

Father Joshua's voice had a dry, crackling quality. "Yes, yes. I recall we were speaking of your son's desire to enter West Point."

"Exactly." Mr. Sheridan wet his lips. Phil, sitting next to him, was acutely aware of his father's nervousness.

Father Joshua had leaned his hands together. His long

fingers, meeting at the tips, formed a sort of roof. "I take it, John," he said, addressing Mr. Sheridan by his first name, "that there has been a development."

"Yes, Father." Again Mr. Sheridan wet his lips and moved slightly in his chair. "Phil has received his appointment. He may enter the Academy next summer—unless, unless, of course, it is wrong for him to go."

"Wrong?" It was Father Dominic speaking. His was a rich, ringing voice that raised echoes in the small room. "Why shouldn't Phil go to West Point? What could possibly be wrong about that?"

"Everything!" The sharpness of Father Joshua's reply made all of the others jump a little. "If Phil spends the next four years at West Point," the older priest continued in his crackling voice, "there is a very good chance that he may lose his faith."

Father Dominic's eyes widened. "Am I hearing you correctly?" he asked. "Did you say 'lose his faith'?"

"Such was my expression."

"But how? How could that happen?"

"West Point is a denominational school."

Father Dominic stared, amazement all over his pleasant features. "But, my good brother," he protested, "have you forgotten that West Point is a tax-supported school and that the First Amendment to the Constitution forbids such institutions to favor one religion over another?"

"Nonetheless . . ." Smoothly, one of Father Joshua's hands sailed through the air. "Nonetheless," he repeated, "there is only one chapel at West Point, and, as you know, it is not Catholic. Few of the students are Catholic, and the whole atmosphere is such that I fear it may prove harmful. I repeat— if Phil spends four years at West Point, there is a very strong chance that he will lose his Catholic faith."

Father Joshua turned to Mr. Sheridan. "And now, John," he said, "what is it you want from me?"

"Your advice, Father," replied Mr. Sheridan in a weak voice.

"My advice, eh? I will give it to you in three simple words: Keep Phil home!"

Mr. Sheridan started to speak again, but for the time being no words came.

As for Phil, he knew not what name to give the feelings inside himself, because there were two of them—and one was as strong as the other. On the one hand, he knew that if he did not get to go to West Point he would die of disappointment. On the other, he knew that if the priests and his father forbade him to go and he went anyhow he would die of shame. And alongside these feelings was still another—a growing feeling of anger. Not anger at his father or at the priests; not anger at anyone or anything in particular; just anger! He gripped the arms of his chair, remembering how many times his mother had lectured him about controlling his temper.

"Careful now, Phil," he told himself. "Careful now, careful!"

Mr. Sheridan had found his voice. "But, Father Joshua," he was saying, "you know my son. You know how it is with him. Since he was knee-high to a grasshopper he has wanted to be a soldier. And those weren't just boyhood fancies, Father; Phil is the same to this day. To be a soldier is his goal and West Point is his dream.

"And now, Father," he went on earnestly, "you tell me to keep him home. But if you do, I'll have a caged lion in my house. So I ask you—what am I to do with this boy?"

"Do!" The dry, crackling voice shot back. "Do with him,

John? I'll tell you what to do. Rather than send him to West Point, take him out into the back yard, behind the chicken coop, and cut his throat!"

"But Phil's dream . . . " Mr. Sheridan stopped short, jumped to his feet, then turned and left the room without another word.

Phil had risen. His eyes moved from one priest to the other, and it was like looking into different worlds. Worry and sternness came back to him from Father Joshua. Pity and compassion were in the face of Father Dominic.

"Excuse me, please, Fathers." With great effort Phil kept his voice under control. "I'll go after him and make sure he's all right."

He hurried from the room, but when he got outside there was no sign of his father. Mr. Sheridan, moving fast, had already disappeared over the side of the hill.

Phil went only as far as the lowest of the porch steps. Actually it was not a desire to go after his father that made him leave. It was the fear that if he remained he might say something harsh to Father Joshua, something that he would regret as long as he lived.

The feeling of anger was terrible in him now. There was a wrought-iron railing down the steps. He moved over and took hold of it, squeezing it. The bite of the iron into his flesh hurt. He was glad of that. He continued to squeeze the railing with all his strength. As the pain grew in his hand, the greater pain of the anger ebbed from his heart.

Shortly it was gone. He was about to move on when the door opened behind him.

Phil spun around. It was Father Dominic. He came down the steps quickly and rested a hand on Phil's shoulder.

"I'm glad you're still here," he said. "But there! If you

weren't, I would have run after you. My brother and I have been talking since you left. Father Joshua spoke out of concern, Phil—out of great concern for you. You understand that, don't you?"

"Of course I do, Father Dominic."

"It's a terrible thing to lose one's faith," the priest said quietly.

Phil nodded. "I know it is," he said. "The most terrible thing in the world."

Father Dominic smiled. "I told my brother that you would say as much," he said. "Now that he has calmed down a bit, my brother asks me to give you this suggestion. Don't be guided by what you have heard here this afternoon. Say your prayers, and let God guide you. Ask yourself this one question: 'If I go to West Point, will I be strong enough to keep the faith that is in me?' And if the answer is yes . . ." Father Dominic ceased speaking. He looked hard into the young man's eyes. There was a silence.

Phil broke it. "Father Dominic," he said, "I can give you the answer to that right now. The answer is yes."

"Then go, Phil. Go! And take our blessing— mine and Father Joshua's—with you!"

★ ★ ★ ★ ★ ★ ★ ★ ★ ★ ★ ★ ★ ★

5

WEST POINT

On a summer afternoon in 1848 Phil Sheridan stepped from a small steamer onto the plankings of a dock on the western shore of the Hudson River in upstate New York, shouldered his baggage and started up the steep path to the sun-drenched plateau above.

Reaching the hilltop, he lowered his baggage for a while and gazed around. A warm breeze coasted through some nearby elms. Lifting his eyes, Phil could see in the distance the open fields and the indigo hills, fold on fold of them, that overlooked the brightness of the river. But his interest was less in these than in his immediate surroundings. He was having his first look at West Point.

On his way east he had talked with a man who knew the United States Military Academy well and who had described it. Consequently, as he picked up his baggage and moved on, he could put names to much of what he was seeing.

Spreading away to the horizon on his right was the Parade Ground, the Plain as it was called. Encircling its 41½ acres was a carriage road. Off this, mostly to the south, stood the main buildings.

Phil trudged eastward, along the southern segment of the road. First, on his left, was the Academy itself, the three-story stone building that housed the classrooms. Next came another stone building, the Mess Hall. At the comer, where the road curved northward past the little houses occupied by the Superintendent and other officers, was the largest building of all, a four-story, L-shaped structure with red sandstone towers and a sally port for entrance.

This was the Cadet Barracks. Here, in a sparsely furnished room, fourteen by twenty-two feet in size, Phil would spend much of his time during the years ahead. . . .

They were full and sometimes difficult years. For a boy brought up in the easygoing atmosphere of a small Midwestern town, the strict ways of West Point were not readily cottoned to. It sometimes seemed to Phil that there were so many rules and regulations that a fellow couldn't take a breath without breaking at least six of them. And every time you broke a rule and got caught at it, down went one or more demerits on your conduct roll. These demerits became permanent black marks on your service record. If you got too many of them, you were expelled and sent home.

One regulation forbade a cadet to leave the premises without permission from the War Department in Washington. But to this regulation there was an important exception. On Sunday, Phil and his fellow Catholics were permitted to attend Mass in the neighboring village of

Highland Falls. There were very few Catholics at the Point, so it didn't take the priest at Highland Falls long to count the uniforms in his congregation. On Monday he sent off a report to West Point. Whenever a cadet skipped Mass, four new demerits found their way into his conduct roll.

Although Phil got a few more demerits than his share, those for missing Mass were not on the list. Phil's faith remained strong.

The young cadet had no trouble with the military part of his schooling, and when in his second year cavalry training began in earnest, he was in second heaven. He loved horses, always had, and was at home on them.

He did have trouble with the academic requirements, however, with such subjects as French and with what was called "English grammar, including etymological and rhetorical exercises, composition, declamation and geography of the United States."

He also had some troubles of another sort. The cadet uniform consisted of a stiff single-breasted gray coat with tails, gray trousers with a black stripe at the sides, white gloves, a high-crowned black hat with an eight-inch black plume and a leather cockade. On Phil's stubby frame this rather garish outfit did not show to advantage. However well fitted, his uniforms always looked as though they'd been thrown at him rather than put on.

Such was not the case with those members of the cadet corps who came from the South. Brought up in the gracious atmosphere of Southern plantations, these young men wore their uniforms with an air. They looked like good soldiers whether they were or not, and most of them were; at any rate they got the best marks and received the majority of such honors as West Point had to offer.

Among these elegant young men Little Phil, accustomed to friendly and democratic Somerset, was ill at ease. Their proud manner produced in him a dislike for the Southern aristocracy, a dislike that would stay with him for the rest of his life.

It seemed to him that the Southern cadets acted as though they owned West Point. Probably some of them thought they did. After all, the Superintendent, Robert E. Lee, was a Southerner. So was Robert S. Garnett, the Commandant. So was George H. Thomas, instructor in cavalry and artillery tactics. So, as a rule, was the ranking cadet captain, the student commander of the battalion into which all of the cadets were formed.

Phil's "pet peeve" among the Southerners was William Rufus Terrill, a Virginian. Young Terrill was a well-set-up young man. He had good looks. He had charm. He had intelligence. He also had, in Phil's opinion, a sneer in his voice.

Ordinarily the military day ended with an evening dress parade on the Plain. It was during one of these ceremonies that there occurred an incident that would be long talked of among the cadets—an incident, furthermore, that would prove a turning point in the life of Phil Sheridan.

It was a September evening. Young Terrill was a cadet sergeant, in charge of the unit with which Cadet Sheridan was drilling. The members of the unit were at attention and Sergeant Terrill was putting them in shape for the parade. His order was to dress in a certain direction.

Phil executed the order promptly and snappily. In his opinion he was now exactly in the position he was supposed to be in.

Sergeant Terrill thought otherwise. Calling out Sheridan's name, he repeated his order.

Phil was furious. It wasn't so much that Terrill had questioned the correctness of his position. It wasn't that Terrill had singled him out by name. Both of those things had happened before. It was that sneer in Terrill's voice. It was the Southerner's arrogant and imperious manner.

Phil began to argue. Terrill silenced him with a warning, repeating his command in a voice of steel.

Everything inside of Phil went to pieces. It was 1851, the beginning of his fourth year at the Academy. For months on end he had kept a tight rein on his high spirits, struggling to chalk up a good record for himself. Now suddenly his temper broke loose from the leash on which he had fastened it.

Sergeant Terrill was standing some six paces away. Phil covered the ground in a breath of time. What's more he covered it with his bayonet lowered. Another step and the point of the bayonet would have entered Sergeant Terrill's body. Just one more step!

But Phil did not take that last step. Something stopped him—as though an invisible hand had suddenly arisen in the midst of the red haze in which he moved, to hold him back.

The incident did not end at this critical moment.

Sergeant Terrill, as was his duty, reported Phil to the authorities. Angered, Phil made up his mind to get even. The two encountered one another, some evenings later, in front of the barracks.

Phil attacked with his fists. Much the larger of the two, Terrill was no mean fighter. Phil was within an inch of getting the thrashing of his life when a regular officer of the Academy came around the corner, broke up the fight and ordered each youth to send a letter of explanation to the Commandant.

Nothing, of course, happened to Terrill. Since Phil was

Phil attacked with his fists.

the attacker, his case was taken under advisement for several days. They were miserable days. What Phil had done, he realized, could mean his dismissal from West Point, the end of his military career.

But he was not dismissed. He was suspended and sent home, with orders to report back the following August.

Awaiting him in Somerset was his old job at Finck and Dittoe's—and almost twelve months in which to do some thinking. Nothing much was said about the incident by his family. His mother welcomed him with a bear hug, Mary and his younger sisters with a kiss, his father and the boys with hearty handshakes. But nobody asked embarrassing questions or delivered any lectures.

Phil was grateful for that. It helped him to think—and he had considerable thinking to do. He did a great deal of walking, in the evenings after work or on Sunday afternoons. Sometimes he dropped into the little brick house on Academy Hill to chat with the priest-brothers. It was a pleasure to hear Father Dominic's rich chuckle again, to have Father Joshua admit in his dry voice that he was glad now Phil had decided to go to West Point and that he hoped when he got out he would be the greatest general there ever was.

Determined not to waste his time, Phil also did some studying. He boned up on the subjects that had given him trouble at West Point.

One August afternoon, in the summer of 1852, he was reading at the kitchen table. The other members of the family were out in the yard. Now and then he could hear his father's rumbling voice or his sister Mary's high laugh.

Laying his book down after a time and looking up, his eyes came even with the calendar above the fireplace. It came to him that this was the last Sunday he would sit thus in the kitchen. Next Sunday he would be on his way back to West Point.

Through the open door drifted his mother's musical tones. She was saying something— he couldn't make out what—to the others. And suddenly he wasn't in the kitchen any more. Suddenly he was a small boy again, walking with his mother and Mary to church in the cool of a spring morning.

Phil knew that this was only an old memory coming back, but for a few minutes the memory was stronger than reality. It was as though he *were* a restless nine-year-old again, as though he and his mother and Mary *were* walking together along the orchard path.

His mother was doing most of the talking. She was telling them why the cannon was booming on Reading Hill. It was because the Vice President of the United States was coming to Somerset that noon. Now she was laughing her beautiful laugh, and the next minute she was dead serious. She was asking Phil what he meant to be when he grew up, and he was telling her that he was going to be a general.

And his mother was saying, "Don't generals fight battles, and don't they fight to win—to get victories?"

And he was saying, "Naturally."

And his mother was saying, "Very well then. You listen to this, my fine young bucko, and listen well. Before you win any victories over anyone else, you're going to have to win a little victory over yourself. You're going to have to learn how to control that temper."

Phil gave his head a shake, shaking away the past as he did so. Picking up his book from the kitchen table and rising, he was startled to discover that Mrs. Sheridan had come in from the yard. He wondered how long she had been standing there, gazing at him as he daydreamed.

She smiled as their eyes met. "Well now," she said, "I don't know when I've seen you looking so grave and serious-like. It's grand thoughts must be running through your head."

"Nothing worth mentioning," he said. Walking across the room, he gave her a hug.

"Whisht now!" She drew back in surprise. "What's come over you? I was right then. You do have something on your mind."

"As I said, Mama," he told her, "nothing much."

As a matter of fact, he had a great deal on his mind. Phil Sheridan had made a decision. He couldn't just throw away his temper. It was part of him. It was part of the way God had made him. But from now on, he promised himself, he would always control it.

★ ★ ★ ★ ★ ★ ★ ★ ★ ★ ★ ★ ★

6

THE SECRET OF THE FROWNING FOREST

Young Phil returned to West Point determined to complete his studies and realize his dream of becoming a military officer. He succeeded in keeping out of trouble and was graduated with the West Point class of 1853. On his first assignment he was sent to the Pacific Coast to fight hostile Indians. The outbreak of the War between the States found him in Oregon with the 13th Infantry. Traveling east on orders, he spent almost a year as a desk officer, first as commissary for the Union forces in southwest Missouri, and then as quartermaster in the campaign that a few weeks earlier had brought a large Union force—the Army of the Mississippi—to Corinth, Mississippi, twenty miles north of Booneville, a little railroad-junction town in the northeastern section of the state.

Eager to see real fighting, Phil had no liking for desk soldiering. Shuffling morning returns, requisition papers and bills of lading was irksome to a man of his spirited temperament. But Phil was being true to the promise he had made to himself in the kitchen of his Somerset home that last Sunday before he returned to his studies after his suspension from West Point. He practiced self-control now, and always would.

In short he had become a good soldier. He did whatever job was handed him to the best of his ability.

His diligence as a desk officer had attracted the attention of his superiors. Soon some of them were saying that Phil Sheridan should be given a command in the field. Among those who recommended this was General William Tecumseh Sherman, the same Cump Sherman who, during Phil's boyhood, had come so often to Somerset to court the attractive Ellen Ewing, now Mrs. Sherman.

Phil's reward came on May 25, 1862. He was appointed colonel, placed in command of the 2nd Michigan Cavalry and ordered to Booneville with his and another cavalry regiment. Fourteen days later he went up another notch. Although not yet of brigadier-general rank, he was given command of both regiments, his own and the 2nd Iowa. The two regiments together constituted a brigade.

In the beginning Phil's men didn't quite know what to make of their new colonel. They looked him over. Then they looked at one another. Then they said, "He doesn't *look* like a soldier." They didn't let it go at that, for they were reasonable and fair-minded fellows. "We'll give him a month," they said, "and see what he's made of."

It didn't take a month. They began to get an idea of what Little Phil was made of even as they began their journey to Booneville.

Ordinarily the cavalry, going from one place to another, moved at a trot. But no sooner was the trek under way than a strange order came back through the long column under Little Phil's command. His soldiers were to dismount and lead their horses at a walk.

There was consternation in the ranks.

What kind of crazy order was this? the men wanted to know.

Important work was awaiting them at Booneville. Their mission was to drive out the Confederate troops guarding the Booneville railroad junction. Then they were to break the railroad line itself so that the Confederates, fleeing before the Federal Army of Mississippi, couldn't make use of it. But with twenty miles to travel and this addlepated colonel ordering them to walk and lead their horses— shucks, the whole blasted war would be over before they got there!

But it wasn't. They not only got there in plenty of time, but, after their pleasant, leisurely jaunt, they arrived as fresh as daisies and as full of snap as firecrackers. In a series of short, spirited forays, they routed the small Confederate force from the village. Then they ripped up a mile or so of track, heated the rails and made bow ties and horseshoes of them by bending them around tree trunks.

Once all these things were done and the brigade had gone into bivouac north of the town, the men began having second thoughts about their little colonel.

Maybe, they decided, he wasn't so addlepated after all. They began to see why he hadn't let them burn up the roads en route to Booneville. He wanted his men and their horses fit when they reached the battlefront. No point tiring themselves out on the way. "Besides," offered a husky, six-

farmer from Michigan, "we got here just as quick as we ld have if we'd made a dash of it. Seems like the fastest way to get to a place is to go there slow." Which was about the way Colonel Phil himself had it figured.

As the days rolled on and the brigade put out its pickets and patrols and settled down to guard work, the men began making more discoveries about their commanding officer. With every new discovery their respect for him mounted until, in many cases, it became adoration.

Phil was considerate of his soldiers. "Men," he said, "who march, scout, and fight and suffer all the hardships that fall to the lot of soldiers in the field, in order to do vigorous work must have the best bodily sustenance and every comfort that can be provided." So ran his military gospel. He applied it not only to his men but to their horses. Especially to the horses. Phil wasn't too hard on a soldier who turned out for inspection a little disheveled. But woe to the man whose mount needed a grooming or looked as though it had not received its proper share of forage!

His mother's training had not been wasted. He was a bear cat on cleanliness. Every morning he would tear through the camp, cautioning and scolding his men.

"All right now," he'd shout, "let's get this place policed. Let's keep it clean. If I find a speck of trash in a company street, the officers of that company won't be officers an hour hence. The same goes for you noncoms. Hop to it or somebody else will be wearing your chevrons. Hop to it, I say!"

The men hopped and loved him for making them do so. The six-footer from Michigan put into words what all them were thinking. "By crickety," he said, "it's good to learn that an army camp doesn't have to be a pigsty and smell to high heaven."

The young farmer might have been even louder in his praise had he known what was happening all over the country. In Federal and Confederate camps alike more men were dying of disease produced by unsanitary conditions than were dying in the hard-fought battles of what, before it was over, would be the bloodiest and most costly war the world had yet seen.

The chasing away of a few Confederates and the breaking of the railroad line did not end the brigade's job in Booneville. The railroad junction was an important point. Sooner or later, as everyone knew, the Confederates would be back in an effort to recapture it.

Against that day, the day of battle, Little Phil made ceaseless preparations.

Neither now, nor later on, was Phil a rear-echelon commander. He always fought up front, under fire, riding along the line on a big horse, hollering at his men, bawling them out, spurring them on.

Because of this colorful behavior he would soon have the reputation of being reckless. As a matter of fact he was no such thing. Sheridan never sent his cavalrymen charging into the face of enemy fire just to make a good impression. He didn't believe in sacrificing lives needlessly. He didn't believe in sacrificing them at all unless he had reason beforehand to think that there was something to be gained by doing so.

He himself could put on a lavish show of dash and bravado—but he did so only because he realized that that was the best way to put heart into his men and to keep them fighting. Dash and bravado, in themselves, had little to do with making him the great military leader he became.

What then was the quality, the main quality, that did? In all truth it was the very same quality that, at the early age of

Phil always fought up front.

seventeen, had made him a good bookkeeper at Finck and Dittoe's Dry Goods Store in Somerset, Ohio.

The secret of his success was careful preparation, slow and thoughtful planning, and elaborate attention to detail.

At Booneville, waiting for the Rebels to attack, Phil sent his scouts all over the area with orders to reconnoiter it inch by inch. He had brought with him some maps of the region. Even if they had been good, he wouldn't have relied on them. As it was, they turned out to be worthless. Soon he was tossing them aside and creating a detailed information map that he kept handy at all times.

He kept his scouts hard at it. He insisted on knowing the location of every back road and cowpath, every hill and swamp, every farmhouse and outbuilding. How many streams were in the vicinity? Where were they and through what territory did they flow? How much water was in them at this season? How much was likely to be in event of rain?

The six-footer from Michigan wasn't so happy about this phase of things. "By crickety," he grumbled one evening, returning to bivouac after a weary day of reconnaissance, "it wouldn't surprise me none if the Colonel had us count every weed in that old cotton field down there where the Blackland and the Booneville roads meet at the western edge of town!"

There was a forest flanking the Blackland road, the main road coming into town from the West. This forest was the outstanding landmark in the area. One of the Yankee soldiers encamped at Booneville had called it the "Frowning Forest" and the name had caught on. Frown it did; it was a mean place, dank and close under its thick-set trees.

The Frowning Forest caught Phil's attention from the start. Beginning at the edge of town and extending along the Blackland road for three and a half miles, the forest was dark and thick. An enemy force, creeping through it, could come right up to the outskirts of Booneville before being seen. That is, if the forest could be penetrated at all—but could it?

Even as he pondered this question, an idea took form at the back of Phil's mind as he sat at his table in front of his tent. He laid the map that he was drawing on the table and summoned one of his officers, Captain Alger.

"Look here," he said, drawing an index finger along the map, "there's the Blackland road coming straight in from the West. Now suppose the Confederates come along that road?"

"Suppose they do?" said Captain Alger, a handsome, dignified-looking man, older than Phil. Now commanding a company of Michigan cavalry, he later would become governor of his state and for a time Secretary of War in Washington, D. C.

"Well then," Phil replied, "perhaps we'll make use of the forest."

"How?"

"I'll tell you how. We'll put our battle line at the edge of town, right near the juncture where the two roads meet. We'll keep the enemy busy there. Meanwhile, we'll send a force of men, three or four companies, through the forest. Those men will take a wide curve and come out again on the Blackland road three and a half miles west of town. They will then be at the enemy's rear, and that will be the end of him."

"It's a good idea," Captain Alger conceded, "if—"

"Go on," said Phil, who knew very well what the "if" meant. "A good idea if—what?"

"If it's possible for any human being to get through that forest."

"That," said Phil, "is what we've got to find out."

The next day he ordered a detail of men into the forest with one of his best corporals in charge. The detail had a tough go of it. The air under the tall trees was hot and fetid. Moving through it was like moving through wet gauze, and everywhere there were swarming gnats and buzzing mosquitoes. Where the earth was more or less solid, the brush was so matted, the vines and briars so clinging that for considerable distances the men had to cut and whack a path for themselves. Mostly the bottom was swamp or at best treacherous mud. Every few steps one man or another sank to his knees, and had to be helped out. Then came the quick, frantic business of rescuing the boot or boots he had left behind him.

But the corporal and his men did get through, and that night the corporal made an excited report to Colonel Phil.

There was a way through the forest. There was an old wagon road. "A weedy old lane," the corporal called it. The lane swept wide through the swamp and came out onto the Blackland road about where the forest ended west of town.

This was good news, but there was a hitch.

Having found the lane once and having followed it, the corporal and his men were not at all sure they could ever do so again.

The Colonel frowned. He took to pacing up and down the length of the Sibley tent. Before the War between the States was over, Little Phil would pace in this manner a good thousand miles. He thought better on his feet, in motion, so up and down he went, a frown clouding his features.

In battle, he realized, speed was important. There would be no time, when the guns started spitting and flaming, for his soldiers to grope and hunt their way through the forest. Up and down he went, in even, steady strides.

Captain Alger was standing toward the rear of the tent. Little Phil came to a sudden halt, facing him.

"There's only one thing to do," he asserted. "We'll have to find a guide. Surely in Booneville or in the nearby countryside there's a man who knows the forest and who's willing to cooperate with Union soldiers. Do you think you could snoop around a bit, Captain—taking care, of course, that no one catches on to what we're thinking—and perhaps find me such a man?"

"I'll do my best, sir."

After three days of careful snooping, Captain Alger ran into luck. Loafing about in one of the local stores, he overheard a group of people talking about a farmer called Beene. "Just the man we need," the Captain told himself, hastening out of the store on his way to the Beene farm. There, after some conversation with the man, the Captain was certain Beene was the guide they sought.

Accordingly, the next morning, he sent two soldiers out to bring Mr. Beene into the Union camp.

On this morning of June 26, 1862, a yellowish mist clung to the lowlands in the vicinity of Booneville. At brigade headquarters, seated at the table in front of his tent, Colonel Phil was studying the map of the area that he himself had drawn up.

He grunted occasionally. Once he scowled. Shortly, getting to his feet, he took up a pair of field glasses and walked to the edge of the hill.

Adjusting the glasses, he trained them on the Frowning Forest. For some seconds Phil let his gaze remain where it was. Then, shifting position slightly, he examined the smaller Booneville road.

As Phil returned to his table, Captain Alger crawled out of one of the pup tents set up near the larger Sibley tent which was Sheridan's headquarters. The man rose to his feet and there was an exchange of salutes.

"Good morning, Captain Alger," said Phil.

"Morning, sir." Before speaking again, he took a deep breath of the muggy, early-morning air. "Perhaps you already know this, sir," he said, "but I sent a couple of soldiers off at dawn. They're bringing in that farmer I talked with yesterday."

"Good." Plying a pencil, Phil made some changes in his map. "What is the farmer's name again?"

"He pronounces it as though it were Beany. It's spelled B-E-E-N-E."

"And you talked with him quite a bit yesterday?"

"I did, sir."

"What do you think? This is pretty tricky country around here. Our soldiers could use a good guide. But this man Beene, does he appear to be the right man for the job?"

"I think so, sir. He's a man of about fifty, I'd say. Of course, it's hard to tell. The land around here isn't too good and these farmers have a pretty hard struggle of it. Sometimes they look older than they are."

"True, true." There was a touch of impatience in Phil's voice. "But does Mr. Beene know the country?"

"He should, sir. He's lived here all his life."

"And the woods?" Phil nodded in the direction of the Frowning Forest. "Could he guide our soldiers through there if it became necessary?"

"He says he knows it well. When I told him our men called it the Frowning Forest, he chuckled. He said it wasn't as bad as all that— not when you get to know it."

"I see." Phil's voice hardened. "And Mr. Beene's sentiments?" he inquired. "We need a guide badly, but we can't use Mr. Beene if he's a Rebel at heart. He won't do if he's secretly working for the Confederate Army."

Captain Alger shrugged. "He says he's a Union man."

"And the townspeople who told you about him?"

"They say he is. Some of them won't speak to him. In their eyes he's a traitor to the Southern cause."

"What do you think, Captain?"

"I think Mr. Beene is telling the truth. However, he'll be here shortly, sir. You can question him. Once you've done that, I expect you'll know whether he's a Confederate spy or the Union man he calls himself."

"Let's hope so."

Phil lowered his eyes to the map lying on the table. The years had wrought no striking changes in his appearance. Now at his full height, he stood a little short of five feet five inches. He was still wiry and long of arm, a black-haired, swarthy-skinned, awkward little man.

The blue uniform of a Union officer fitted him no better than had the "monkey suit" of his West Point days. The one he was wearing had only recently been a captain's uniform, onto the shoulders of which he had hastily stitched the newly acquired eagles of a regimental colonel.

The Captain was the first to notice the return to camp of the two soldiers he had sent to fetch Mr. Beene. He dismissed them quickly, after they had made their report, and beckoned to the tall, lanky man who had ridden in with them.

Mr. Beene had a sallow face, sleepy eyes and tawny-colored hair. He took his time as he dismounted from a saddleless white nag and joined the officers. There was a chaw of tobacco in his mouth, and to this he was devoting most of the little effort he seemed inclined to put forth.

"Howdy," he said, taking little Phil's hand as Captain Alger made the introductions, "Always glad to meet another Lincoln soldier."

Phil indicated a camp stool across the table from his own, and Mr. Beene took it. Captain Alger remained standing.

Phil fired his first question fast. He hoped that Mr. Beene, caught off guard, would answer without stopping to think. In that case he would know quickly whether this skinny, slow-moving Mississippi farmer was a Union man or only pretending to be one.

"Mr. Beene," he said, "do you think the Southern states had a right to secede from the Union?"

This attempt to jolt the farmer into sudden speech was wasted. Mr. Beene sat and chawed for some time before opening his mouth.

Even then he didn't speak. He sailed a stream of tobacco juice through his teeth. If his goal was the flat white stone some ten feet distant, his aim was good. The shiny, golden blob went straight to the stone and splattered.

Next the lanky farmer leaned forward, planting his elbows on the table. "Begging your pardon, Mr. Colonel," he said, "but I've got one bad ear. Now I heard most of your question. You asked me was it right for the Southern states to do something from the Union. It's that 'something' I didn't quite catch. Seems like there's one word there I didn't quite hear."

"The word was 'secede,' Mr. Beene."

Mr. Beene indicated that he had heard this time by a nod of his head. Then he chawed some more.

Phil began to wonder. Was this man a little hard of hearing, as he claimed? Or was it possible that he did not know the meaning of a word that was currently on every American's lips?

"Mr. Beene," he said, speaking loudly and clearly, "you do understand the word 'secede,' do you not?"

"Oh, sure, sure, sure." Mr. Beene chawed some and continued. "For a state to secede from the Union," he said with great deliberation, "is for that state to leave the Union and set up its own government or join up with some other or both."

Mr. Beene paused long enough to send another spray of tobacco juice splattering over the flat white stone. "Now," he proceeded, "you want to know what I think about secession. Was it right, you want to know, for the Southern states to secede?"

At this point Mr. Beene seemed to feel he should rest a little before going on, which he eventually did. "The way I see it, Mr. Colonel," he said, "whether the Southern states had the right to secede or not don't make no never mind. After all, a man has a right to do a lot of things that he oughtn't to do. Take me, for instance. I'm a married man with children— lots of children. All right, now, I got a right to whip those youngsters of mine every day of the year if I want to. But I don't do it. Right nor no right, I figure all that whipping ain't good for them. 'Tain't good for me either when you come right down to it. Well ..."

Mr. Beene, falling silent, took another rest. "Well," he continued in time, "that's the way I feel about this secession thing. Maybe the Southern states had a right to do it. Maybe they didn't. Either way, they shouldn't have. What they did was bad for the country as a whole. The way I see it, Mr. Colonel, if this country is going to be big and happy and strong, we all got to stick together. After all, North or South,

East or West, we're all Americans, and when these here Southern neighbors of mine up and decided to quit being Americans, they made a big mistake."

The tall farmer removed his elbows from the table and folded his arms. "There you are, sir," he finished. "You've asked me my beliefs and I've done told you. Now what kin I do for you?"

Phil glanced at Captain Alger. The Captain smiled. Phil did the same. The farmer's words rang true. "I believe, Mr. Beene," Colonel Phil said quietly, "that Captain Alger has given you a pretty fair idea of what we'd like you to do for us."

"Sure has," agreed Beene. "Sure has. And I kin do it, Mr. Colonel. I kin lead your soldiers through the Frowning Forest, as you call it, any time you say the word."

"Then there's only one thing more. I want you where I can put my hands on you at a moment's notice. You'll have to live here in camp until—well, until our Confederate friends decide to pay us a visit. Is that all right with you?"

"Tis," said Mr. Beene with a chaw and a nod. "I don't mind camping out a mite. Just when do you think the Confederates will be coming?"

"Who knows? Tomorrow maybe, the next day, maybe the day after that."

★　★　★　★　★　★　★　★　★　★　★　★　★　★

7

THE BATTLE OF BOONEVILLE

But the Confederates did not show up the next day or the next or the day after. It was not until the hot, moist, blinding-bright morning of July 1 that Sheridan's pickets, far out to the west, sighted gray-uniformed cavalrymen moving toward Booneville under command, as was learned later, of General James R. Chalmers.

The first courier galloping in from the picket line had little information to pass on to Colonel Phil and his aides. But almost at once there were more couriers pelting up the hill to brigade headquarters. With them came additional information.

General Chalmers' men were approaching along both the Blackland and the Booneville roads. How many were there?

It was too soon to say. So far the enemy had shown only the heads of his columns. Did the Rebels mean business; were they going to attack? That, too, remained to be seen.

Bending over the table in front of headquarters, Little Phil scribbled orders as fast as he could manipulate a stubby pencil. Mounted messengers flew, carrying instructions to the officers in charge of the various elements of his brigade.

Commanding the pickets, out west, was Lieutenant Leonidas S. Scranton of the 2nd Michigan. Dismounting and fighting on foot, Scranton and his men moved slowly back, finally forming a battle line in a thicket where the Blackland and Booneville roads converged at the edge of town.

Even as the first bullets bit the morning air, rolling up a small thunder in the west, more couriers were pounding up the hill to brigade headquarters. In less than half an hour, Colonel Phil had a pretty good line on what he was up against.

The situation wasn't exactly good. Neither was it exactly bad. It was a little of both.

The Confederates were going to attack. No question about that. Nor were their forces as small as had at first been supposed. General Chalmers had with him in the neighborhood of five thousand cavalrymen.

Little Phil had 827.

He was outnumbered five to one.

But over and against this disadvantage were four advantages—four good cards, so to speak; four trump cards, if he played them right.

One "good card" was the lay of the land, the terrain Phil had been at such pains to reconnoiter. His front line, now in position where the two roads joined, was thin. It would remain so for sheer lack of manpower. But it was well anchored on its right by the Frowning Forest and on its left by another tree-thick swamp. There was, therefore, only a relatively narrow area, a sort of funnel through which General Chalmers could pour his five thousand horse-borne fighting men. If Phil's battle line held —if!

So much for the first of his good cards. His second was of a different nature. Colonel Phil, hastily scanning the reports pouring into headquarters, made a discovery.

The Rebels were launching their attack with caution. They were advancing slowly, feeling their way. This could mean only one thing. General Chalmers, their commander, had no idea that Little Phil had so few men. For all the Confederate commander knew, Booneville was bursting at the seams with Yankee soldiers.

Here was a state of affairs that Colonel Phil could turn to good use. He proceeded to do so as fast as he could circulate the necessary orders. Every member of the brigade, from Lieutenant Colonel Hatch, second-in-command, down to the lowest private in the ranks, was to start yelling. He was to keep on yelling till he ran out of breath. Then, when he got his second wind, he was to start yelling all over again.

At the same time Little Phil sent his military band into action. The musicians were to parade at the rear of the battle line. Every man was to get as much racket out of his instrument as the instrument could produce.

"Noise! Let us have noise!" These were Phil's orders. Perhaps he was remembering the Bible stories his mother had told him in his boyhood: How the walls of Jericho fell before the trumpets of the Israelites. He knew, of course, that mere racket would never stave off a force five times bigger than his own. But perhaps 827 men, making all the racket they could, would lead the enemy to think that the Federal forces were far larger than they were.

The third "good card" was even better. The Rebels were armed for the most part with single-loading carbines. Each of Phil's men had one of the new Colt revolving pistols and one of the new Colt revolving rifles. Each Yankee could fire twelve shots before reloading. Card number three then was greater firepower.

And card number four was the Frowning Forest, and the lane winding through it. Plus, of course, the presence in the Yankee camp of Mr. Beene, the skinny, tawny-haired, tobacco-chewing Mississippi Union man who knew the forest and who stood ready to guide Sheridan's men through it if that became necessary.

If it became necessary!

Since his bookkeeping days in Somerset, Phil had been reading military history. During a battle, he knew, it was unwise for a commander to weaken his position by splitting up his forces. If he had to send soldiers through the forest, his plan was to send four saber companies, with Mr. Beene guiding them and Captain Alger in command. He dreaded doing it. The absence of the four companies would further reduce his already dangerously thin line.

"No," he told himself, "no!" He would hold off sending men into the forest. Granted that the hidden lane there was the strongest of his good cards, he would not play it unless he had to.

All morning and well into the afternoon, the battle raged. The Confederates, charging across the cotton field, hit the center of Sheridan's line. Thrown back in hand-to-hand fighting, they embarked on a different tactic. They made a series of flanking movements, striking first at the Federal right and then at the left.

Movement and din were everywhere: the earsplitting

The battle raged most of the day.

chatter of rifles, and steel smiting steel. The gagging smoke of battle caused the Federal line to falter and sway. Again and again it was broken at points and then rapidly mended by the throwing in of reserves. Again it faltered, swayed and fell back. And again!

By midafternoon the Federal situation was bad. Before long it was rapidly going from bad to worse.

Late in the afternoon Colonel Phil saw that his line could not hold much longer. His only chance was to play his last good card—and hope for the best!

He lost no time rattling off his instructions to Captain Alger. The Captain and the four saber companies were to get through the forest as quickly as possible, and come out on the Blackland road three and a half miles to the west and at the rear of the enemy.

"The second you reach the road," Colonel Phil told the Captain, "strike at the enemy's rear. Don't scatter your men. Don't deploy. Charge straight up the road in column. When you attack the enemy's rear, my forces here in Booneville will attack his front."

"One minute, sir!" Captain Alger's lifted hand riveted Phil's attention. "How will you know when my men and I reach the Blackland road?"

"Cheer! Cheer at the tops of your voices."

"And if you don't hear us?"

Phil had considered that possibility. "I'll give you an hour," he said. "When the hour's up, I'll attack here at Booneville whether you've made it through the forest or not. Here's hoping we both strike at the same moment."

"Here's hoping," were the last words of Captain Alger as he rode off at the head of his men.

In the years ahead, Phil Sheridan would lead whole armies

into battle. He would command thousands of men in some of the most crucial campaigns of the war. All the same he would never again know an hour more tense than that which he now experienced in the little Mississippi town of Booneville in the summer of 1862.

His men were taking a terrible beating. He himself was in the midst of things now. Back and forth he rode, across the front line, waving his hat in his clenched fist, shouting encouragement at his soldiers, calling on them to hold on, hold on!

Only seconds before the hour was up, there was a piece of luck. A small train, bringing forage for the Federal cavalry horses, clinkety-clanked up what remained of the railroad track. Seeing it, Phil sent a messenger flying to the engineer. He was asked to keep his steam up and to blow his whistle, thus adding to the racket that Phil hoped would continue to deceive the furiously battling Confederates.

The hour ended. Phil gave the order to charge. He had no idea whether Captain Alger and his men had got through the forest or not. As yet he had not heard the cheering for which his ears were straining.

Again fortune was with him. At the very instant that Phil and his men attacked the enemy front, Captain Alger and the four saber companies reached the Blackland road and hit the enemy rear.

Panic seized the Rebels, sending them off in what at first seemed all directions at once. In truth there was only one direction they could go—out into the fields and away from Booneville, putting all the distance they could, as fast as they could, between themselves and the pursuing Federals.

The day was ending. Darkness was already spilling over cotton fields, over the little hills and woodlands. Four miles west of town, the fleeing Confederates entered a wide-spreading swamp, and Colonel Phil ordered a halt. He knew better than to risk his small force in a tricky area that the Rebels knew well but about which he knew very little.

So ended the Battle of Booneville. It wasn't a battle, as such things went in the War between the States, of course. It was just an engagement, a skirmish. But it had significant results: it held an important point for the Union and it put Phil Sheridan on the map. When news of the victory reached far-off Washington, the worried men responsible for the whole of the Northern war effort rolled a new name off their tongues.

"Phil Sheridan?" they said. "Phil Sheridan? Now just who is he, and why aren't his military abilities being put to greater use?"

★ ★ ★ ★ ★ ★ ★ ★ ★ ★ ★ ★ ★ ★

8

A WORD WITH LINCOLN

During the remainder of the war the North made ample use of the talents of Phil Sheridan. Promoted to brigadier general, and shortly after that to major general, in command of an army corps, he fought in a series of major engagements in the West.

On October 8,1862, he was at Perryville in Kentucky. No victory for either side, the Battle of Perryville was a Northern gain. The Confederates were forced southward, and had to give up an attempt to overrun Kentucky.

For Phil, Perryville was the scene of a memorable incident. Wandering about on the night before the battle itself, he suddenly spied a familiar face in the flickering light of one of the campfires. It was William R. Terrill, the same Terrill whom Phil had nearly run through with his bayonet and whom he had attacked so savagely in front of the Cadet Barracks at West Point. Although a Virginian, Terrill was fighting with the Union as a brigadier general. There was a split second of embarrassment and hesitation. Then Phil stuck out his hand and Terrill grabbed it. Next day Phil was more than happy that he and his old enemy had made up. During the fierce fighting at Perryville, General Terrill was killed.

On September 19 and 20, 1863, Sheridan and his soldiers were fighting at Chickamauga Creek, near Chattanooga, Tennessee. Those were sad days for the North. The Federal Army was defeated. It might have been destroyed had it not been for the holding action of General George H. Thomas, another Southerner fighting for the Union and one of the North's greatest soldiers. Sheridan and his men took part in the heroic last-minute stand that won for Thomas the picturesque nickname of the "Rock of Chickamauga."

And on November 25 of that same year, still in the neighborhood of Chattanooga, Phil and his command fought at Missionary Ridge. There, led by Sheridan and some other officers, the men in blue, acting without orders, scrambled up the steep ridge in the face of searing enemy fire to seize the Confederate positions on top in one of the bravest and most spectacular charges of military history.

So stood Little Phil's record when on March 23, 1864, he received a telegram that puzzled him. It read:

Lieutenant-General Grant Directs that Major-General Sheridan Repair to Washington and Report to the Adjutant-General of the Army.

Why, Phil wondered; why was he being called to the National Capital?

He would have his answer soon.

The War between the States, although no one knew it yet, was entering upon its last twelve months. In after years, most historians would agree that the decisive battles, those which gave the victory to the North, were fought in the West. The groundwork for overthrowing the Confederacy was laid in such campaigns as those which ended at Vicksburg, Mississippi, and at Chattanooga. Even so, the closing campaigns—with one exception—would take place in the East. Among them would be the Atlanta Campaign of General Sherman who, by marching through Georgia and then through the Carolinas, would put an end to all effective resistance to the Union in the deep South. The only exception to the fighting in the East would be the unsuccessful effort made by General John Bell Hood of the Confederate Army to retake the West by sweeping into Tennessee.

In the end, the outcome of the war finally would be determined by two armies facing one another in Virginia. One was the Army of the Potomac under General Ulysses S. Grant. The other was the Army of Northern Virginia under the great Confederate warrior, General Robert E. Lee.

And it was in Virginia that General Phil would put the finishing touches on his own part in the War between the States. As he learned, en route to Washington in the spring of 1864, he had been placed in charge of all cavalry, some 10,000 men, attached to Grant's army.

Phil was now in his thirty-third year. He had lost weight in the hard fighting in Kentucky and Tennessee. His uniform flapped about him like the garments of a scarecrow. On the train bearing him east, some people sitting too far away to see the two stars on his shoulder straps took him for a sergeant on furlough.

Some time before, at Rienzi, Georgia, a man had presented him with a magnificent black horse. The horse had a reputation for being almost unmanageable. Phil named him Rienzi, rode him without difficulty and in short order man and beast had become fast friends. Dashing about on Rienzi, in the storm and flash of battle, Little Phil cut a startling figure. As one of the war correspondents put it, he seemed at such moments to be carrying "the forked lightning in his hands." But once the fighting ended, once he left the battlefield, Phil laid aside all such magnificence. He laughed and chaffed with his aides. Or he simply sat and stared into space, his narrow eyes half-closed, looking a little sullen like a boy who has stayed up past his bedtime.

He had never been in Washington before. As he left his train on the morning of April 4, 1864, he took an instant dislike to the place. His general impression, as he moved about the city making official calls, was that Washington was a town of too much bustle and too little accomplishment, too many important-looking people doing too many unimportant things.

One of his first calls was at the War Department in its dingy red-brick building just west of the White House. There, in obedience to orders, he talked with General Henry W. Halleck, Chief of Staff. Halleck, in turn, took him around to another office to have a talk with a strange and hard-to-understand man.

This was Edwin McMasters Stanton, Secretary of War. The Secretary was a pudgy, quick-moving man with small hands and feet. A streak of white ran down the center of his black, heavily perfumed beard. His eyes were unforgettable: cold and piercing behind their thick-lensed glasses. Little Phil found his manner standoffish and overbearing.

As the conversation jerked and bumbled to its end, Phil told himself that it was one he would not remember with pleasure. He was also depressed by his next conversation—a conversation that took place a few minutes later in a rather shabbily furnished second-floor room in the southeast corner of the White House.

As he stepped into this room, Phil did what he always did in new places. Looking about, he made a quick rundown of whatever he saw.

It was a fairly large room, twenty-five by forty feet. There was a white marble fireplace with brass andirons and a high brass fender. He noticed some chairs, two hair-covered sofas and a long oak table. In the south wall, tall windows looked out on a sweep of lawn, the one-third-finished Washington Monument in the near distance.

Between the windows was a small writing table. From an armchair behind it, as Little Phil entered, a tall man unwound himself. He came hurriedly around the desk and seized Little Phil's hands in both of his.

"Welcome to Washington, General, and to your new command," said Abraham Lincoln.

"Thank you, Mr. President," said General Phil.

They sat down and talked.

"Grant," the President said, "speaks highly of you, General. I hope you will fulfill his expectations."

A long sigh came at the end of these words. The President, Phil could see, was tired to death—a weary, troubled man with eyes that were sad and humorous at one and the same time.

"Thus far," the President continued after a short pause,

"Welcome to Washington, General," said Abraham Lincoln.

"the cavalry you are about to take over has not done all it might have done."

Another sigh, longer than its predecessor. Then the President fell to speaking about cavalry in general. There was a common saying that the cavalry was the safest place a man could be in the army. Lincoln mentioned this and repeated a popular joke. "Who ever saw a dead cavalryman?" he asked with an unconvincing chuckle.

Phil stiffened. He had heard that Mr. Lincoln was a very funny man, but that tired old joke was not at all funny. Not to him. He had seen too many cavalrymen die in too many battles.

He felt uncomfortable, not only because of the little joke, which he knew the President did not really mean, but for another reason. He could feel Lincoln's expressive eyes on him. The President was studying him, he realized, sizing him up.

To date, as Lincoln had just remarked, the cavalry had not given a good account of itself in Virginia. It had proved no match for the Southern cavalry operating there. Several experienced Union generals had been sent into Virginia in an effort to remedy this situation.

Phil knew all this, and he could guess the thoughts running through Lincoln's mind. Lincoln was saying to himself, "If all those fine-looking generals could do nothing to improve the cavalry in Virginia, how can this little man, who doesn't even look like a general, do any better?"

Phil might have been even more uncomfortable had he heard Lincoln talking about him some time after his departure from the White House. Asked to describe Sheridan, Lincoln replied : "I will tell you just what kind of chap he is. He is one of those long-armed fellows with short legs who can scratch his shins without having to stoop over."

Mr. Lincoln was a deeply worried man. He was heartsick at the bloodshed and suffering of the war. He was desperately looking for good generals, generals who could fight hard and fast and get the terrible thing over with. When a month or so later Little Phil began winning battles all over the place, Lincoln was beside himself with joy. He had been mistaken about the little man with the long arms, and no one was happier to admit that than himself.

"What about Sheridan!" he cried when a visitor to the White House made mention of the little general. "Oh," Lincoln went on, his tired face ablaze with pleasure, "Phil Sheridan, he's all right!"

★ ★ ★ ★ ★ ★ ★ ★ ★ ★ ★ ★ ★ ★

9

IN THE VALLEY

President Lincoln's statement that the cavalry of Grant's Army of the Potomac had not been doing well was no news to Phil. He had known as much for some time, and en route to Washington he had thought through a scheme that he believed would alter things for the better.

Heretofore the Union cavalry in Virginia had been used mostly for guard purposes. Bits and pieces of it were forever being sent off to this place or that with instructions to watch over this railroad bridge or that ammunition dump.

Phil had no objections to his horsemen doing some guard work, but he wanted them to do less. His theory was that the cavalry would become an effective part of Grant's army only if, for the most part, it were kept together and trained as a fighting unit.

Army leaders often take a dim view of change and when Phil made his plans known he ran into opposition.

The protests were loudest in Washington. Chief of Staff Halleck shook his massive head. General Halleck had written books on military strategy and tactics. He had read just about all the books on those subjects that he himself had not written. Nowhere, he said, had he read anything to suggest that the cavalry should be primarily a fighting unit instead of a guard unit.

"After all," General Halleck asserted in his smooth and courteous way, "we have the infantry to do the fighting."

Little Phil had an answer to that.

As he saw it, a cavalryman was an infantryman "with four detachable legs." According to Phil, the main purpose of the cavalryman's "four detachable legs"—his horse—was to get him to the battlefield as speedily as possible. Once there, no law said he could not dismount, tether his horse at the rear and do his fighting on foot.

Even General Grant was doubtful about Phil's idea, but he had great faith in the little cavalry leader himself. Sheridan, in his opinion, was "one of the ablest generals" in either army. There were discussions between the two men, even some arguments, with stocky, grubby-looking Grant gnawing at his cigar and Phil pacing back and forth; but in due time, Grant told Phil to try it.

"Mind you," he said, "your idea had better work."

It worked. A few weeks and half-a-dozen battles later, Phil Sheridan's cavalry had become one of the hardest-hitting units of the Army of the Potomac.

Grant, at this point, was hammering away at General Lee's Army of Northern Virginia. Lee was outnumbered, desperately low on supplies and equipment. It would be hard to say, indeed, just what the Confederate soldiers were fighting with in Virginia—with courage mostly, and on nerve.

Inch by inch, Grant pounded southward in what would be known as the Wilderness Campaign because of the tangled brush, the dense forests and the sucking mud over which it was fought. Inch by inch, desperately battling back, Lee retreated.

There was a limit to how far the Confederate leader dared go. At all costs he must keep the Federals from seizing Richmond, Virginia, capital city of the Confederacy. Late June of 1864 found him at the end of his string. Digging in at Petersburg, a little town south of Richmond, he threw up fortifications and stood pat. Grant established his headquarters at City Point on the James River, northeast of Petersburg, and set up his army along Lee's front. Thus began the long and grueling siege of Petersburg.

In August Phil was given the most important assignment he had yet received. He was placed in command of an independent army and told to go into the Shenandoah Valley and bring it under Union control.

Now what was the Shenandoah Valley—or rather what is it—and why was its seizure so vital to the North?

The valley runs for well over eighty miles along the western fringe of Virginia. Beginning near the pleasant town of Staunton it takes a northeasterly course to the bank of the Potomac River, in the neighborhood of Harper's Ferry northwest of Washington. To move southward toward Staunton, in the language of the valley people, is to go up-valley; to move north, toward the Potomac, is to go down.

Two mountain ranges make a corridor of the region. Rising along the west are the Alleghanies, along the east

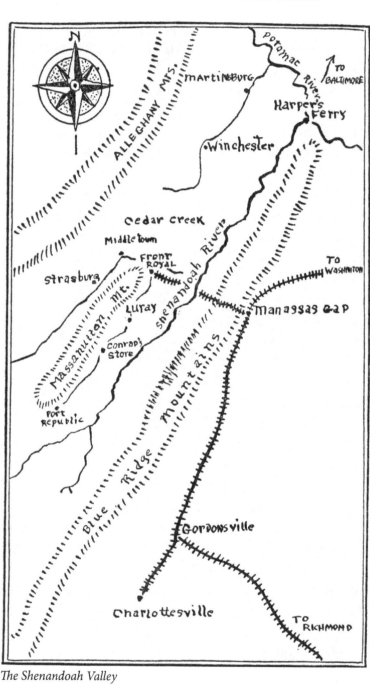

The Shenandoah Valley

the Blue Ridge. About halfway up, in the valley itself, is a smoke-colored ridge, forty miles long, called Massanutton Mountain. Branching around Massanutton, the valley turnpike runs more or less straight down the center of the valley. Running roughly parallel to it is the Shenandoah River. It too branches on reaching Massanutton. Sparkling across the valley at the north or down-end of Massanutton is a little stream called Cedar Creek.

From the beginning of the war, the Shenandoah Valley was one of the Confederates' best assets. From its rich farms streamed carloads of grain to feed the Southern armies. Sheep and beef cattle grazed on the grassy slopes of its hills. There was no more fertile area in the world. And when the summer sun was on it and the grain was tall and the wind moved through it and the cloud shadows cast by the mountains moved over it, there was none more beautiful. Wherever the eye roved, it was met by bulging barns and well-kept fields.

The valley was not only a granary for the South. It was also a protected tunnel leading straight to the heart of the Union— straight, that is, to the outskirts of Washington, D. C.

Down the valley in July of 1864 swung fifteen thousand veteran Confederate troops led by hard-bitten, long-bearded Lieutenant General Jubal Early. For two days, "Old Jube" and his soldiers menaced the fortifications of the National Capital. They made no attempt to capture the city, knowing that their forces were too small to hold it. But, coming and going, they ravaged the rolling farmlands of Maryland and Pennsylvania, and they struck terror into the hearts of Washington's citizens.

Several times topnotch Union generals had been sent into the valley with orders to take it over. None had been able to do so. Now Sheridan was going in with an army of forty thousand. Would he succeed where so many others had failed?

Grant's instructions were harsh.

"Send the enemy retreating up the valley," he said, "and follow him to the death."

And that was only the first half of his order. Grant put the other half in words that would become famous.

"Make all the valley . . . ," he told Sheridan, "a desert as far as possible. I do not mean that houses should be burned, but all the provisions and stock should be removed, and the people notified to get out." Writing to Halleck in Washington, Grant was even more forceful. Sheridan and his army, he wrote, were to "eat out the valley . . . so that crows flying over it for the balance of the season will have to carry their provender with them."

Phil obeyed his instructions to the letter. Moving slowly but steadily up-valley, he and his men stripped the area of every growing thing. In September two battles sent "Old Jube" and his Confederates hurtling northward toward Staunton. Pursuing vigorously, the Federals took positions on a low chain of hills overlooking Cedar Creek.

In October Phil was summoned to Washington on official business. His last orders, before leaving, were for one of his regiments—the 17th Pennsylvania Cavalry—to accompany him as far as the town of Winchester, fifteen miles down-valley. There the 17th Pennsylvania was to go into bivouac and await his return.

Back in Winchester by the middle of the month, he spent the night in one of the tents set up by the Pennsylvanians on a rise of ground south of town. The next morning, the nineteenth, got under way in the customary manner. Shortly before sunrise the bugles sounded boots and saddles. This was followed by the usual stir—men feeding their horses, cooking their breakfasts, making preparations to strike their tents and move south to the Federate' main camp on the uplands behind Cedar Creek.

By nine o'clock General Phil was aboard his big, black horse Rienzi, heading up the valley turnpike. Moseying along beside him were Major Forsyth, one of his aides, and Major Spera, commanding the 17th Pennsylvania. Behind them came the cavalry regiment, moving in column.

The day was sunny with an Indian summer haze in the air. Autumn colors brightened the wooded slopes in the distance. Little Phil jogged along easily, enjoying the balmy breezes, the bantering conversation of his companions.

Major Forsyth was the first to rein in his mount, a startled exclamation passing his bearded lips as he did so.

"Do you hear?" he inquired.

Phil had already tugged Rienzi to a halt. Dismounting in silence, he put his ear to the ground. He kept it there some time before quickly returning to his saddle.

"Gunfire," he said, frowning. "Any idea, either of you, what it could mean?"

Major Spera suggested that "quite likely one of our units is making a reconnaissance in force. Perhaps they've come across an enemy picket."

Major Forsyth was speaking the minute the other officer finished. "We're in a very strong position at Cedar Creek," he declared. "Surely the enemy would think twice before attacking us there."

"He might think twice or even three times," Phil said grimly. "And then he might decide to try it. Move ahead a bit, will you, Major Forsyth? See if you can find out what's going on."

Major Forsyth was not gone long. Shortly he could be seen returning, his horse at a mad gallop.

"It's a rout!" he shouted as soon as he was within hearing distance. "An absolute rout! Our men are coming this way as if the devil himself were at their heels."

General Phil was speaking rapidly to Major Spera, the cavalry commander. "Let me have fifty of your soldiers," he was saying. "We'll go ahead. As for the rest of your regiment, spread it across the valley—clean across. Tell your men to act as traffic police. Make sure they understand what they're to do. They must stop all the soldiers coming from Cedar Creek. And that isn't all. They're to see that every man jack of them turns around and rejoins the battle."

Seconds later Phil himself was streaking south, up-valley, with the fifty escorts the Major had hastily summoned out of the ranks. Rocking along at a steady pace, their horses ate up the miles.

Major Forsyth had not exaggerated. It was a rout all right. The enemy had attacked some time before dawn. Clambering up out of a deep gorge alongside the Cedar Creek camp and swarming through it, the Rebels had grabbed eighteen cannon and thirteen hundred prisoners before the startled Yankees could shake the sleep out of their eyes. Taken by surprise, Sheridan's men had lost their heads.

At first an attempt had been made to carry off equipment, but only at first. For miles now along the approach to the camp, the valley was strewn with abandoned wagon trains, gun caissons and even knapsacks.

Sheridan went forward at top speed. As he neared the camp site, he began weaving from one side of the road to the other, bellowing at his fleeing soldiers, shaming the panic out of them.

"Back!" he shouted. "Back! Back! What's got into you? Are you going to let a bunch of already-beaten Rebels chase you all the way into Winchester? Is that the tale you're going to pass on to your grandchildren! Back! Back, I say!"

They went back!

Men who had spent all their breath and thought they could never run again turned and ran—in the direction from which they had come.

Back they went in what in a matter of minutes was no longer a rout but a swift advance of determined men.

Back they went with Little Phil yipping and hollering behind them and finally, when the battleground was overtaken, charging through them, hat in hand, to the front.

Back they went, in one of the most astounding recoveries of the War between the States. By late afternoon the Battle of Cedar Creek, a smashing defeat for the Yankees in the morning, had become a smashing victory.

Back they went to write what for all practical purposes was the final chapter in the story of the conquest of the Valley of the Shenandoah.

★ ★ ★ ★ ★ ★ ★ ★ ★ ★ ★ ★ ★ ★

10

THE LAST OF THE GREAT CAVALRYMEN

After the Battle of Cedar Creek, Phil's work in the Shenandoah Valley was what military men call a mopping-up action. By late February the remaining Confederate forces in the area had been destroyed or driven out and Phil was on his way to the headquarters of General Grant at City Point on the James River.

In Petersburg, twenty-one miles southwest of City Point, General Lee and the Army of Northern Virginia were still holed up. Around Petersburg in a horseshoe-like arc, the Confederates had set up a line of fortifications over thirty-five miles long. Running more or less parallel with these, the Yankees had set up their own fortifications, an intricate maze of trenches, parapets and breastworks.

At one or two points the rival works were so close that the men in gray and the men in blue could talk to one another. As the weary months piled up, their talk became more and more friendly. Pretty soon they were firing more jokes than bullets at one another and swapping good-natured insults.

The weather was wretched and had been most of the time since the start of the siege months before. There were rains, and then more rains. The pickets sloshing through the gummy mud began to wonder if they would know how to walk on solid earth, assuming that someday the siege were ended and they would have a chance to try it.

"What this army needs," a waterlogged Yankee declared, "is not a Grant but a Noah." Another, putting his hand to his forehead and surveying the swamplike scene, wondered just "when our gunboats will be coming up?"

On and on the siege continued. General Sherman, his march through Georgia and the Carolinas completed, came and went at City Point. Occasionally a steamer called the *River Queen* rolled up the James with President Lincoln aboard. Then there would be conferences, with Lincoln and Grant and Sherman anxiously discussing the problem about which the whole North was talking.

The South was on its last legs. Everybody, North or South, knew that. But there was something else everybody knew. The South wasn't beaten yet. It wouldn't be, it couldn't be, until General Lee's Army of Northern Virginia was either destroyed or compelled to give up.

Somehow, someway, Lee must be forced to move out of Petersburg into the open where Grant's army could get at him. And when Lee moved, care must be taken that he didn't move too far. Down in North Carolina was another Confederate army under General Joseph E. Johnston. If Lee broke loose, if he escaped into the west and joined with Johnston—then the Union leaders would be faced with a new and even graver problem.

The North was war-weary. To be sure a few Northerners wanted the conflict to continue because they were making money out of it. There are always such people around for obvious reasons. Wars come and wars go, but greed goes on forever.

But generally speaking the Northerners were sick of the whole thing. If Lee escaped, the war might drag on for another six months. Then the people of the North might just give up. They might insist that their Government sign a treaty of peace with the South, any kind of treaty, just so long as it put a stop to the bloodshed. Then the Federal Union—the Union for which almost three hundred thousand Yankees had already died, the Union established by the Founding Fathers—would be gone forever.

The Northern leaders had to act, and they had to act fast. The question was what to do.

The answer revolved around a railroad line that entered Petersburg from the West and was usually spoken of as the Southside Railroad. The importance of this line was that it was the only one still in Lee's hands. As long as the Confederate General could hold onto the Southside, he could bring supplies into Petersburg—ammunition for his guns, food for his men and forage for his horses. And as long as he could bring in supplies, he could stay where he was.

So all the problems confronting the Union leaders were really one problem. The Southside Railroad must be seized. At the very least it must be threatened. Then Lee would have to move out of Petersburg. He would have to act to protect his one remaining supply line. Otherwise he and all the Confederates in Petersburg would be faced with starvation.

The Union leaders made plans and threw them away. They made more plans and threw them away. Then, at long last, they went into action.

Late in March, Phil led a cavalry force of some thirteen thousand south and west around General Lee's fortifications. His destination was a Virginia hamlet called Dinwiddie Court House. The plan, once Sheridan was in position near Dinwiddie, was for him to strike north toward the Southside Railroad tracks, some ten or twelve miles away. An anvil-and-hammer operation, the plan would be termed in later years. Phil, whipping around Lee's right flank and threatening the railroad, was to supply the anvil against which Lee would be forced to throw at least a portion of his army. Once Lee began to move out of Petersburg, Grant was to close in on him from the east, thus supplying the hammer blow.

There were two big clashes. The first was in the neighborhood of Dinwiddie. The second, taking place on the first of April, 1865, was somewhat to the north where five roads met at a point called Five Forks.

At Five Forks it was Sheridan against George Pickett, one of the South's finest generals. Sheridan had his cavalry, augmented by sixteen thousand infantrymen. Pickett had a powerful combination: five brigades of infantry and almost all of Lee's cavalry.

It was a day-long battle, and one to remember. Sheridan fought as always, riding all over the field on his big horse. An infantryman fighting beside him was struck full in the throat, and the man pitched to the ground.

"You're not hurt a bit," Sheridan roared at him. "Pick up your gun, man, and move right on!"

The soldier did what thousands of Sheridan's men had done before him. He obeyed his commander. He picked up his gun, drew himself up, staggered a dozen steps—and fell, dead.

Evening colors were already in the sky before Sheridan launched the attack for which he had been putting his men in readiness since early morning. When the time came, he called for his battle flag, a small, two-pointed banner bearing the stars of a major general. Banner in hand, he rode his horse over the enemy breastworks and plunged forward, a riotously yelling infantry at his heels. At the same moment, moving according to plan, another segment of his forces struck at one of the enemy flanks.

The Confederates broke, recoiled briefly, broke again.

The last great battle of the War between the States was over.

The railroad was in Union hands now. Lee, hurrying out of Petersburg with the rest of his army, had no place to go. Grant was smashing at him from one end; Phil's forces lay across his line of retreat at the other.

On the morning of Sunday, April 9, 1865, General Philip Henry Sheridan and some other Union officers sat their horses, a small knot of silent men, on a roadside near Appomattox Courthouse in central Virginia.

The sun was out, a welcome sight to men who in recent months had seen enough rain to last them for a lifetime. The damp grass was silver at its tips, and a breeze played among the new leaves along the tree limbs.

It was Palm Sunday. Little Phil had gone to Mass early. He still carried his palm, and somewhat nervously, from time to

On a roadside near Appomattox Courthouse.

time, he moved it from one hand to the other and back again.

After a while the man for whom the officers were waiting came along the road, his horse at a gentle gait. It was General Grant, looking a little woebegone in a mud-spattered uniform.

He stopped his horse and nodded in the direction of the nearby village of Appomattox. His words were addressed to Sheridan.

"Is General Lee up there?" he asked.

Sheridan said yes, he was.

Grant said, "Very well, let's get up."

All around, in the fields, stood the men of the two armies— the blue and the gray. They weren't saying anything. The only sound, as the officers trotted off, was a Yankee band playing "Auld Lang Syne."

Within an hour the telegraph wires were spreading the news. General Lee had surrendered.

That night—Palm Sunday night—General Grant, sitting in his headquarters, was startled by the sound of gunfire. Alarmed and distressed, he hurried out.

What was the meaning of that noise? he asked some aides standing nearby.

He was told that his soldiers were celebrating.

Celebrating what? he wanted to know.

The surrender, of course, he was told.

General Grant didn't think the surrender of so gallant a man as General Lee called for any festivities. He saw to it that the guns were silenced.

"The war is over," he told his troops. "The Rebels are our countrymen again."

Now that the fighting was over, there came a period of American history known as the Reconstruction.

It was a troubled period. The bad feelings between North and South—the very suspicious and misunderstandings that had helped bring on the war in the first place—were only increased by the war itself. Nor did they fade away the minute the guns fell silent. For some time the South remained under what amounted to Federal military control. During a portion of this period, Phil administered the military Division of the Gulf and later was made Governor of a military district embracing Louisiana and Texas.

Still later he was sent to Chicago where for a number of years, as head of the Department of the Missouri, he directed operations against several hostile Indian tribes, finally forcing them to settle on the reservations specified in treaties their chiefs had made with the United States.

In 1869 he was promoted to lieutenant general and in 1888 to full general.

He was married in 1875. His wife, the former Irene Rucker, was the daughter of an army officer. Theirs was a happy marriage. Phil was a loving husband and a devoted father. There were four children: Mary, the first-born; Irene and Louise, who were twins; and Philip Henry, Jr.

Phil spent the last year of his life, 1888, with his family at the resort town of Nonquitt, Massachusetts, writing his memoirs. He finished them on the second of August. Three days later he was dead.

The solemn requiem Mass was sung at St. Matthew's Church in Washington, D.C. James Cardinal Gibbons delivered the sermon, and thousands came to pay homage to a man who, in the not distant future, would be known as the last of the great American cavalrymen.

Among the priests taking part were two brothers from the Midwest. Father Joshua and Father Dominic Young were old men now, old men with long memories. They had taught General Phil his catechism and watched him grow from little boy with big temper to little man with big self-control. Their prayers for the boy they had known were fervent and their hearts were full.

ABOUT PHIL SHERIDAN

Sheridan's Ride

UP from the South at break of day,
Bringing to Winchester fresh dismay,
The affrighted air with a shudder bore,
Like a herald in haste, to the chieftain's door,
The terrible grumble, and rumble, and roar,
Telling the battle was on once more,
And Sheridan twenty miles away.

And wider still those billows of war,
Thundered along the horizon's bar;
And louder yet into Winchester rolled
The roar of that red sea uncontrolled,
Making the blood of the listener cold,
As he thought of the stake in that fiery fray,
And Sheridan twenty miles away.

But there is a road from Winchester town,
A good, broad highway leading down;
And there, through the flush of the morning light,
A steed as black as the steeds of night,
Was seen to pass, as with eagle flight,
As if he knew the terrible need;
He stretched away with his utmost speed;
Hills rose and fell; but his heart was gay,
With Sheridan fifteen miles away.

Still sprung from those swift hoofs, thundering South,
The dust, like smoke from the cannon's mouth;
Or the trail of a comet, sweeping faster and faster,
Foreboding to traitors the doom of disaster.
The heart of the steed, and the heart of the master

113

Were beating like prisoners assaulting their walls,
Impatient to be where the battle-field calls;
Every nerve of the charger was strained to full play,
With Sheridan only ten miles away.

Under his spurning feet the road
Like an arrowy Alpine river flowed,
And the landscape sped away behind
Like an ocean flying before the wind.
And the steed, like a barque fed with furnace ire,
Swept on, with his wild eyes full of fire.
But lo! he is nearing his heart's desire;
He is snuffing the smoke of the roaring fray,
With Sheridan only five miles away.

The first that the general saw were the groups
Of stragglers, and then the retreating troops;
What was done? what to do? a glance told him both,
Then, striking his spurs, with a terrible oath,
He dashed down the line 'mid a storm of huzzas,
And the wave of retreat checked its course there, because
The sight of the master compelled it to pause.
With foam and with dust the black charger was gray;
By the flash of his eye, and the red nostril's play,
He seemed to the whole great army to say,
"I have brought you Sheridan all the way
From Winchester, down to save the day!"

Hurrah! hurrah for Sheridan!
Hurrah! hurrah for horse and man!
And when their statues are placed on high,
Under the dome of the Union sky,
The American soldier's Temple of Fame;
There with the glorious general's name,
Be it said, in letters both bold and bright,
"Here is the steed that saved the day,
By carrying Sheridan into the fight,
From Winchester, twenty miles away!"

—THOMAS BUCHANAN READ

Union officers: Sheridan, Merritt, Gregg, Davis, Wilson, Tobert

Sheridan's Circle

This monument in Washington D.C. commemorates the victory of Sheridan's army over the Confederates at Cedar Creek. Sheridan had left his troops in the Shenandoah Valley and traveled to Washington D.C. Upon his return he found his army retreating against a surprise attack from Jubal Early's Confederate troops. Sheridan rallied his men from their retreat and returned them to the battle. The Confederates had stopped to rest and loot the Union camp, having effectively won the battle, and were caught by surprise by the returning Union army. It was a decisive victory for the Union and ended forever the Confederate invasion of the North. Sheridan's mad ride from Winchester to Cedar Creek is not only immortalized in this monument, but also in the poem Sheridan's Ride.

© Bpperry | Dreamstime.com - <a href="http://www.dreamstime.com/stock-photo-general-phil-sheridan-statue-sheridan-circle-washington-dc-memorial-civil-war-embassy-row-pennsylvania-ave-bronze-dedicated-image57373113#res4917459">General Phil Sheridan Statue Sheridan Circle Washington DC Photo</a>

CPSIA information can be obtained
at www.ICGtesting.com
Printed in the USA
BVHW082021240323
661081BV00014BA/681